W9-AEW-989

Management Information Systems and Organizational Behavior

Management Information Systems and Organizational Behavior

- Pat-Anthony Federico
- Kim E. Brun
- Douglas B. McCalla

PRAEGER SPECIAL STUDIES • PRAEGER SCIENTIFIC

Library of Congress Cataloging in Publication Data

Federico, Pat-Anthony.
Management information systems and organizational behavior.

Bibliography: p.
1. Management information systems.
2. Psychology, Industrial. 3. Management.
I. Brun, Kim E., joint author. II. McCalla, Douglas B., joint author. III. Title.
T58.6.F35 658.4'0388 80-15174

ISBN 0-03-057021-2

Opinions or assertions contained herein are those of the author and are not to be construed as official or reflecting the views of the Department of the Navy.

Published in 1980 by Praeger Publishers
CBS Educational and Professional Publishing
A Division of CBS, Inc.
521 Fifth Avenue, New York, New York 10017 U.S.A.

0123456789 145 987654321

Printed in the United States of America

PREFACE

Modern advances in computerized information technology (for example, large mainframes, mini- and micro-processors, stand-alone and graphics terminals, chip technology, bubble memory, more powerful software, better communications equipment) facilitate the collection, storage, processing, retrieval, and display of data. With the implementation of innovative technology, these operations are performed more rapidly, flexibly, accurately, completely, and economically than ever before. Such improvements in computerized information systems are changing the way both managers and organizations perform. The development of this novel technology has accelerated much more quickly than managers and their organizations have learned to use it. The sudden advent of computerized information systems has generated a prodigious literature regarding its advantages and disadvantages for management and the organization. Given modern managerial methods and ordinary organizational occupations, it is reasonable to expect that computerized information systems will have a noticeable impact on managerial performance and decision making, as well as organizational structure and processes.

A computer-based management information system (MIS) is a computerized procedure for providing managers with immediate access to the knowledge, information, and data they need to make decisions, direct people, and regulate operations in order to better attain organizational goals. This is accomplished by remote-access, time-sharing computers and graphic display devices that give the system its intrinsic capacity to input, process, store, transform, transmit, and output data internal and external to the organization into appropriate formats for use by decision makers. An MIS can be used for reporting systems; monitoring past, present, and future trends; operating systems such as inventory and production control; supporting quantitative systems to manipulate statistical data; programming automated decision systems to make choices under specifiable situations; and implementing simulation systems to yield information depicting possible alternative states of nature that are of concern to management.

Business, governmental, educational, healthcare, and research and development enterprises utilize MISs to facilitate many different tasks (for example, command, control, and communications; strategic and tactical decision making; manpower, personnel, and logistics management; instruction and testing; and medical diagnosis). Considerable effort and expense have gone into the design and development of hardware and software for MISs. However, most executives and their respective enterprises are unaware of the possible and/or actual consequences of implementing these technological systems. The purpose of this volume is to identify and discuss the many implications of MISs for managerial performance and decision making, as well as organizational structure and processes.

The relevant professional literature concerning the impact of MISs upon managerial and organizational behavior is reviewed, integrated, and evaluated. We identify the alleged and actual effects of these systems upon different managerial functions and management levels; organizational structure, processes, and information processing; and executive and organizational decision making. The monograph is organized in two parts. The first deals with the impact of MISs upon managerial performance and decision making; the second deals with the implications of MISs for organizational structure and processes.

Pat-Anthony Federico
Kim E. Brun
Douglas B. McCalla

San Diego, California

CONTENTS

Chapter Page

PART II: IMPLICATIONS OF COMPUTER-BASED MANAGEMENT INFORMATION SYSTEMS FOR ORGANIZATIONAL STRUCTURE AND PROCESSES

1

IMPACT OF COMPUTER-BASED MANAGEMENT INFORMATION SYSTEMS UPON MANAGERIAL PERFORMANCE AND DECISION MAKING

1
IMPLICATIONS OF COMPUTER-BASED MANAGEMENT INFORMATION SYSTEMS FOR MANAGEMENT

PRACTICE OF MANAGEMENT

Attempting to define a computer-based management information system (MIS) is not an easy task. A review of the literature shows little agreement among the many authors. Each interpretation generally mirrors the author's background and biases concerning information and its utilization (Kurz, 1973; Ein-Dor, 1975). This situation is largely a consequence of the fact that there is no solid disciplinary foundation to which MIS can trace its roots. The closest thing to a heritage for MIS is "the integrated data processing of the 1950's and the total systems's approach of the early 60's" (Vazsonyi, 1973a). The lack of agreement as to what constitutes an MIS has undoubtedly deterred many authors from attempting to put forth a specific definition. Instead, they generally offer vague conceptual notions of what an MIS should do, or they attempt to describe the characteristics of an MIS. Still, irrespective of the degree of detail, any definition of MIS should deal with the concepts of management (the means of accomplishing tasks through other people), information (the knowledge communicated between people), and system (the set of related elements or components held together by a common goal) (Neel, 1971).

As early as 1958, Leavitt and Whisler describe the interrelated components of information technology, the forerunner of MIS. At this time, information technology includes computer methods for (a) handling vast amounts of information quickly, (b) applying statistical methods to decision-making problems, and (c) stimulating via computer higher-order thinking. Whisler (1970b) later defines information technology as "the technology of sensing, coding, transmitting, translating, and transforming information." Sprague and Watson (1975) expand Head's (1967) model of MIS and discuss three major supporting subsystems: (a) the structured reporting subsystem, which includes communications with the environment external to the organization and traditional operating reports internal to it; (b) the data base subsystem, which deals with the input, storage, and output of the system, as well as system maintenance; and (c) the decision-making subsystem, which includes decision models, ranging from applications such as inventory control and production scheduling to simulation routines.

In a briefer description, Fredericks (1971) describes MIS as an "interlocking, coordinated set of management systems designed to optimize the planning, control, and administration of specific processes operationally, tactically, and strategically." Burdeau (1974) identifies the major attributes of an MIS as the operating system, the measuring system (which monitors the operating system), the reporting system, and the management system. And Kennevan (1970) states that an MIS "is an organized method of providing past, present and projection information relating to internal operations and external intelligence. It supports the planning, control and operational function of an organization by furnishing uniform information in the proper time-frame to assist the decision maker." Similarly, "a management information system (either computer-based or manual) is defined as a communicative process in which data are accumulated, processed, stored and transmitted to appropriate organizational personnel for the purpose of providing information on which to base management decisions" (Holland, Kretlow, & Ligon, 1974).

Other authors (Greenwood, 1969; Neel, 1971; Ross, 1970) describe an MIS as a system or network of parts designed to provide information flows to the decision maker, so that he may best accomplish the managerial tasks of planning, organizing, and controlling. Finally, Orlicky (1969) identifies the following as essential characteristics of computer-based MISs: (a) a data base, (b) a large amount of data stored in random-access files, (c) a remote two-way communication network between user and system, (d) fast system response time to the user's information requests, (e) flexibility as to the amount and format of data output for both planned and unplanned information requirements, (f) capacity to provide successive levels of detailed analysis of a problem, and (g) a procedure for data-file security.

In an attempt to integrate the broad spectrum of meanings given the term MIS, we propose the following definition: an MIS is a computerized procedure for providing managers with immediate access to the knowledge, information, and data they need to make decisions, direct people, and regulate operations, in order to better attain organizational goals. This is accomplished in conjunction with remote-access, time-sharing computers and graphic display devices, and by the system's intrinsic capacity to input, process, store, transform, transmit, and output data, both internal and external to the organization, into appropriate formats. An MIS can be used in many ways: to report on systems; to monitor past, present, and future trends; to operate systems such as inventory and production control; to support quantitative systems that provide manipulation and statistical analysis of date; to program automated decision systems for making choices under specifiable situations; and to implement simulation systems to yield information depicting possible alternative states of nature that concern management.

For our purposes, the terms management practice and the practice of management will be synonymous. Both refer to any action a manager takes while performing for the organization. The growth of MIS naturally affects the practice of management. In fact, MIS might begin to fill the vacuum that exists, in part, within the organization's communication system (Murdick, 1972).

Several authors perceive basic changes in management practice resulting from the introduction of MIS. Diebold (1969a) and Churchill, Kempster, and Uretsky (1969) think that the complexity, boundaries, and scope of management will increase, as will the quantity of detailed data gathered and applied. These factors singly or jointly would enlarge the manager's workload (Stewart, 1971). In fact, one might conclude that the practice of management would become unwieldy as the amount and nature of the information changes. Daniel (1961) thinks that MIS influences not only what is practiced, but also how well it is done. Eventually, the change in management's environment might result in the modification of behavior. According to Clayton (1973), the role of MIS is to shape management practices by guiding and advising management concerning its information needs. This manipulation of perceived information needs might ultimately alter management practice and management structure.

If in fact MIS does modify management practices, it may be assumed that many of the dimensions traditionally attributed to the practice of management, such as challenge, responsibility, opportunity, and reward, will no longer be present. Anshen (1960) believes that if this "erosion of traditional responsibilities" occurs, then the organization may find it "devastating" in terms of recruiting new employees for management positions. The underlying assumption is that new management prospects will seek organizations providing the previously listed attributes. Of course, this may be a poor presumption, but the problem still exists if MIS changes the practice of management. Uris (1963b) agrees with Anshen that recruitment of managers will change as a result of the introduction of MIS. Uris sees gaps too large for a normal upward mobility from worker level to manager level. He assumes that the filling of these managerial positions will be accomplished by recruitment from outside the organization. External selection of managers could enhance the modification of management practices if only those individuals are hired who meet the recently altered management roles specified by MIS usage. Thus, not only would MIS influence on management practices be realized and perpetuated, but structural changes would also be likely to occur.

In contrast to those who believe that MIS will alter the practice of management, others forecast very little change. Murdick (1972) thinks that the thrust of MIS is toward improving information systems for management application, but that this does not mean that "the computer is going to take over management." It is his belief that MIS may be used for routinizing internal practices, but that, in essence, "good management will have much more effect on the use of the computer than good computer usage will have on management practice." What will change, according to Murdick, is the amount of management time spent concentrating on the more "important problems" concerned with the practice of management. Gilman (1966) agrees that MIS will be "an adjunct to managerial decision making," but he does not think it will shape the practice of management one way or another. MIS will merely assist management to move in the "direction it feels it must go to solve its challenges and problems."

In a later section, we will discuss in greater detail this disagreement concerning the impact of MIS on managerial behavior. For the time being, we merely note that a controversy exists. In the following sections, we are concerned only with areas of actual and/or potential MIS impact.

SPECIFIC LEVELS WITHIN THE MANAGEMENT STRUCTURE

Management of most organizations is divided into separate levels. Each level usually consists of management positions with related responsibilities, job requirements, and control features. Almost without exception, these levels have been dubbed top, middle, and lower. Such stratification assists in defining the impact of MIS upon the individual activities of each group.

Many writers (Gilman, 1966; Karp, 1971; Leavitt & Whisler, 1958; Reif, 1968; Schoderbek, 1971; Shaul, 1964; Whisler & Shultz,

1960) recognize that the impact of MIS will depend on the management level involved. Thus, the introduction and utilization of MIS will not have the same implications for top management as it will for middle or lower management. Leavitt and Whisler (1958) project that the greatest impact will occur in the top and middle management areas, implying that little if any effect will be generated in the lower level. In fact, the top levels, possibly due to the nature of their tasks, have received the most extensive coverage. (We consider the projected and actual implications of MIS for top management in the next section. This is followed by a discussion of the effects on both middle and lower management.)

What influence will MISs have on the jobs of top management? Whisler and Shultz (1960) believe that the "organizational responsibility of top management will remain the same." In other words, top management's loyalties will not be altered as a result of developments in information technology within its organization. But the job content—and thus managerial skill requirements—might change. Greenless (1971) states that increased utilization of time-sharing systems would require a greater number of top managers skilled in the use of computers and other quantitative techniques for analysis and decision making. (The need for reeducation and training to meet new skill requirements of top management is covered in greater depth in a later section.)

The power and control vested in top management may also be in jeopardy as a result of the computer (Field, 1970). Top management might actually be programmed by lower management in such a way that upper management activities proved more apparent than real. Data-reduction could be used to accomplish this "stripping of power from the mighty" (Field, 1970). Field also asserts that if this modification of top management behavior is probable, future decisions could be made by the computer. Not only might this cause a shift in power; it could also eliminate administrators. R. E. McDonald, in Kleinschrod's (1969) article, agrees that organizations may "no longer be efficiently controlled by a chain of command."

Other authors (Karp, 1971; Whisler & Shultz, 1960) do not anticipate this usurpation of power and control, or the programming and automating of top-management jobs. In contrast, the integrative impact of information technology would emphasize systematization and rule development, resulting ultimately in the programming and automating of lower and middle management's (rather than top management's) functions (Whisler & Shultz, 1960). Karp mentions (1971) that computerized systems will greatly benefit the thinking of top management personnel, assisting them to view the organization as an "integrated system," instead of dissimilar functional departments. A systemic view of the organization can improve top management's understanding of the organization and decrease the possibility of any centralization of power outside the designed structure, as defined by top management.

Reif (1968) claims that "the management group which will be most affected by the organization's increasing reliance on the computer is middle management." Traditionally, the function of middle-level managers has been to make routine administrative and control decisions. According to Reif, it is these functions, when integrated with upper management, that require an "interlocking network for management information," that is, an MIS. An integrated MIS could provide better and faster control over these traditional functions and could influence management's power, spreading it widely among many middle managers (Kleinschrod, 1969). In effect, a decentralization of middle management control and power would take place as wider utilization of the MIS occurred. Leavitt and Whisler (1958) agree that a "reorganization of middle management levels should occur." They think that a dichotomizing of the middle management levels would take place, with one large group sinking into a highly programmed state, and the other smaller group becoming more autonomous and more creative in its thinking. This latter group would ultimately become an adjunct to top management, effectively eliminating all power and control middle management might have possessed prior to the introduction of information technology.

Managerial behavior in an MIS environment may also be modified. For example, Leavitt and Whisler (1958) conjecture that the "good guy" or "conformity to get ahead" behavior of junior executives "should become far less significant in a highly depersonalized, highly programmed, and more machine-like middle management world." Conformity in this context does not refer to the constraints that MISs would place on the individual manager in the form of routine limits, program restraints, and possibly decision rules, but rather to the limitation of a superior's mode of operation in order to better one's own position within the organization. As for the MIS-related constraints on behavior, Leavitt and Whisler believe that middle managers, to be able to satisfy those personal needs and aspirations that are stymied on the job, will seek fulfillment outside it, as have hourly workers.

Very little has been published directly commenting on the influence of MISs upon the behavior of lower management. Most work, as noted in the preceding section, has concentrated on the middle manager. Of the articles reviewed, only two attempt to discuss the actual or potential impact of computers on lower management. Shaul (1964), comparing lower-level management to middle management, decides that the middle manager could more easily cope with a transition to electronic data processing, because of his familiarity with "all the ramifications of the information system," or a more globally integrated knowledge of the organization. Lower management, in comparison, usually has a somewhat restricted view of the organization. This is due partly to the time requirements of their jobs. They are typically not kept well informed of the total organization and the many interconnections within the information system.

The other article (Gilman, 1966) deals with an age old problem of the lower-level managers, that of being caught between the worker on one side and upper management on the other. According to Gilman, this is not going to change much. In fact, besides having to cope with this traditional bind, lower management may find itself caught between two sets of computers, one involved with production processes and the other with MIS. Both networks could in turn create separate communications problems: in one case, the translation of computer-based operating instructions to the worker, and in the other the attempt to convey computer-derived decisions to subordinates. In this situation, lower management's only chance to escape, short of leaving the organization, would be to get promoted into middle management and that stratum where many writers see MIS's greatest impact.

The impact of computers on middle management has not yet been settled, but it is sure to be substantial (Schoderbek, 1971). This seems to indicate that although many authors have made projections about the impact of MIS on individual levels of management, little has been done to substantiate and identify exactly what has changed, if indeed anything has. One study that makes such an attempt was conducted by Stewart (1971), who found that "the nature of the effects varied considerably," depending on how the information process was organized and applied. This suggested that one could make only categorical statements concerning the impact of computers on management. But Stewart also found that the effects are not inevitable: they depend in large part on managerial attitudes. Deciding whether or not to use a computer system necessitates a reexamination of management policies and procedures. Stewart's findings shed light on the impact of computer-based systems on specific management levels, but they do not really tackle the MIS itself.

NUMBER OF MIDDLE MANAGERS

Middle management will be the level most affected by MIS. Among other things, these systems are bound to change the number of mid-level managers required within the organization. Almost all of the literature reviewed in this area addresses itself to the impact on middle management, but the various authors come to diametrically opposite conclusions: some say that the number of middle managers will increase in number; others say they will not.

Early in the development of MIS, many authors feel that information technology will definitely reduce the number of middle managers in the organization (Burck, 1964a, 1964b; Kraut, 1962; Leavitt & Whisler, 1958; Lee, 1964). Leavitt and Whisler in their classic article predict that information technology will "allow fewer people to do more work." This, they declare, will cause a reduction in the number of middle managers. According to Lee, the basic assumption here is that the tasks of middle managers will gradually become automated. Kraut claims that if this assumption is correct, then the reduced workload will demand fewer managerial positions, and, correspondingly, a reduction in promotional opportunities. All of this implies a major change in the structure of management and in the organization itself.

In addition to workload reduction, there will also be a decline in the exercise of middle management judgment (Uris, 1963). This decrease in decision making will eventually diminish the size of middle management. Sanders (1969) agrees, but he also thinks that computerization will increase both the rewards and the challenges of these positions. Sanders, in contrast to Uris, asserts that the job content of the future middle manager will increase. This implies that the decision-making responsibility in those positions left after reduction would also increase.

We have summarized the positions of those authors who project a major decrease in the ranks of the middle managers. The views of those writers who oppose this conclusion will be discussed shortly. At this point, it may be pertinent to comment on the fact that none of the articles just reviewed studies this problem directly: they present only projections and conjectures concerning the impact of MISs. Two authors who do look at the real management world are Burck (1964a; 1964b) and Hoos (1960). Both writers agree that the middle-management level is being reduced. In Burck's case, however, the sample was selected from the industrial environment, with the recent installation of a computer system as the criterion for selection. In the few firms sampled, Burck found that these companies had undoubtedly reduced the number of middle managers employed. Hoos confirms Leavitt's and Whisler's forecast. The middle manager's job has either been combined or eliminated altogether. It is also found that the communication system, as well as the decision-making process, has been centralized following the introduction of a computer system and the manager's authority has been visibly truncated. These findings seemed more empirical than Burck's. Hoos had sampled 19 organizations for two years before concluding her study. For this reason her findings seem accurately to represent the impact of electronic data processing systems upon middle managers. However, Burlingame (1961) believes that Hoos' conclusions are "dubious" and "unreliable." He thinks, instead, that organizational decentralization will continue to "grow and flourish" and that the ranks of middle management will correspondingly increase. This argument is based on the premise that decentralization will continue—not necessarily that computerized systems will alter the middle management level. This is also a projection and not a statement of findings.

Uris (1963b), commenting on the new information technology, forecasts some trends. He predicts that executive featherbedding will increase as the organization attempts to ease the shock of technological obsolescence. This trend, if actually realized, would obviously increase rather than decrease the number of managers employed. The trend might also be attributable in part to the young technologically oriented managers, who were hired to occupy the new positions created by these computerized systems. But instead of a "fearsome oversupply of technologically unemployed middle managers," Kleinschrod (1969) found "a serious shortage of competent management personnel."

It turns out that "the computer has opened up far more opportunities for middle managers than it had closed off useful careers." Shaul (1964) finds that although large quantities of detailed, monotonous administrative work will be eliminated, there will be "no accompanying reduction in the need for middle managers." The job requirements of middle managers will also increase in complexity. This implies that new skills and specialization will be needed. Jackson (1970) asserts that these increases can be attributed to a greater demand for middle managers and that "their numbers [could] increase with computer use." Jackson believes that increases in responsibility and subsequent upgrading of the middle management position will lessen the need for top managers: "not only [will] there be fewer top managers, but their decision-making authority [will] be further delegated to the middle management ranks." This article does not, however, back up these statements with empirical data, and is therefore no more conclusive than the many other futuristic articles previously mentioned. The contradictory ideas concerning the impact of MISs upon the size of middle management, although partly resolved by the few empirical studies, suggests that further investigation is needed.

IMPLEMENTATION OF INFORMATION TECHNOLOGY

What is implementation? Leavitt and Whisler (1958) allude to the existence of definable stages in the life cycle of an MIS. Such stages are sometimes labeled planning, purchasing, implementing, and utilizing. Implementation generally refers to the introduction and subsequent use of an MIS whose purpose has been defined in some manner. Implementation is that point in the development cycle of an MIS where it begins to take over the functions it was designed to replace. The planning phase has been completed and the time has arrived when the hardware is brought up to operational levels. Now the organization must begin its adaptation to the new communication system. Implementation is also that portion of the MIS evolution that meets with, and creates, most of the problems for an organization. These difficulties are the topic of the present section.

Leavitt and Whisler (1958) state that the "most compelling reason" for implementing information technology is "the pressure on management to cope with increasingly complicated" organizational problems. They also assert that the temporal distance between the discovery of new techniques for processing organizational information and the practical application of those techniques shrinks at almost a geometric rate. This time constraint has been a major cause of many of the impediments encountered during implementation. Other difficulties include the location of control implementation; the need for re-education of those who interact with the system; alterations in the needs of users; and effects on managerial attitudes and behavior. The need to control or maintain the three systems associated with the introduction of an MIS places significant demands on management (Mann & Williams, 1960). These sequential systems are the old or pre-installation, the transitional or implementation, and the new MIS. Mann and Williams believe that the net result of management's attempt to control these three systems will involve a delegation and/or assumption of duties. This will have the effect of spreading supervisory responsibility among a greater number of managers. Burck (1964a; 1964b), however, thinks that if top management does not take control of the planning and the implementing of computer applications, middle management will resist the changes in organizational structure and job functions, and a crisis will result. So with regard to who should control the implementation of an MIS, there are two prevalent viewpoints: sole responsibility and control should be retained either by top-level management or by lower-level management.

Leavitt and Whisler (1958) identify another hindrance that must be considered prior to, during, and after, installation of an MIS: management's lack of preparation and knowledge of the system and its technology. The transitional period has a tendency to place "heavy stress" upon management's "technical competence and cognitive skills" (Mann & Williams, 1960). If the manager who is to use the system cannot, or will not use it, then the entire project is wasted

(Powers & Dickson, 1973). Cattaneo (1971) claims that the primary problem arises in the design stage, because the system is not usually designed with the manager in mind. He claims that this stems from the technically uneducated manager's inability to communicate his operational demands to the technically educated systems designers. Powers and Dickson (1973) declare that the problem is due to the "tremendous difference" between the factors that make an MIS successful, and the factors that an MIS specialist speculates are important. They suggest the need for a rethinking and further examination of the essential principles and factors required of an MIS. Even if the requirement for training and re-education is recognized, the lack of time for adequate training makes the conveyance of technical knowledge extremely difficult during MIS implementation. Some managers are finding it extremely difficult to keep up with or ahead of their subordinates, who are rushing forward to learn new techniques, jargon, and details of electronic data processing, without any interference from having worked in the old system. This could cause considerable stress if the manager perceives his subordinate's re-education as a threat to his own position (Mann & Williams, 1960). (This is discussed further in a subsequent section.)

During the transition period management must maintain an abnormally high level of communications. More memoranda and more meetings are required because each change may affect interdependent departments in unknown ways. Thus in order to maintain a cohesive and cooperative environment, most implementation-oriented decisions require review and discussion by representatives from each of those departments. More than likely, a participative environment would result in successful implementation and sufficient utilization of the MIS (Mann & Williams, 1960). (The impact of lack of participation will be discussed in a later section.)

The stress of implementing an MIS can be caused by any of the problems previously presented. One issue almost universally associated with any planned project is the failure to meet predetermined target dates. In the transition phase, these dates might represent completion of specific stages, or the final conversion date for the entire system. The pressure produced by internally and externally imposed deadlines is described by Mann and Williams (1960) as the "most serious psychological stress" a manager may experience in implementing an MIS. It occurs because management bases its deadlines on inadequate knowledge and establishes milestones too early in the planning stage. No easy solution has been tendered—only a description of this important problem. Another stressful situation can be created as a consequence of the inherent emphasis information systems place on measures of effectiveness and efficiency. According to Radford (1973), these quantitatively measured criteria could cause managers to believe that their performance will be appraised in similar terms. He recommends the use of participative management, or management by objectives, as a means of circumventing this problem and creating a more amiable environment.

One last problem that directly emphasizes the transition and implementation of an MIS deals with the effect on employees of temporary assignment to new jobs required during implementation. It is believed that the job holder will feel very insecure in these temporary jobs. According to Mann and Williams (1960), such feelings stem from the fact that these workers are at a disadvantage once the MIS is implemented, since they are now forced to compete with other employees for the jobs created by the MIS, and since the requirements of the created positions may exceed their abilities. This problem seems to emphasize again the need for retraining, re-education, and encouragement of participatory control styles. Many more actual or projected problems, and their proposed solutions, will be stated in following sections. Obviously, problems encountered with an MIS are not exclusively confined to that period referred to here as implementation, but occur throughout the range of management and organization interactions with these systems. The problem of participation will be discussed next.

PARTICIPATION OF MANAGEMENT

"Authors, teachers, enlightened managers, and consultants all have stressed the necessity of participation" (Bieneman, 1972). In all phases of MIS—planning, development, implementation, utilization, and maintenance—the involvement of management is essential (Churchill, Kempster, & Uretsky, 1969; Dock, Luchsinger, & Cornette, 1977; Kadin & Green, 1971; Poindexter, 1969). Although the theme of noninvolvement is common, some authors affirm that participation is more essential in a few specific stages of MIS creation than it is in others. Yaffa and Hines (1969) believe that the planning and developing phases are the most critical to system success. They find that the decisions concerning systems configuration are often left up to the equipment manufacturer's sales representatives. As a result, management fails to take advantage of the educational gains inherent in an MIS feasibility study. As they see it, the feasibility study and the involvement of management in the planning and developing phases provide an excellent means of training individuals in the technical and operational characteristics of an MIS. In another study the federal government (NBS, 1966) concludes that "the single most critical problem" is, without a doubt, the "need for understanding and support" by the organization's management.

In a study of the management of computer resources, Churchill, Kempster, and Uretsky (1969) have found not only that newly developed applications require management involvement, but also that the "extensive operations of the computer resource require managerial participation." This implies that Yaffa's and Hines' thesis concerning the limited need of participation may not be the best approach. Rather, management must maintain its involvement and participation throughout the life of the system. Kegerreis (1971) studies a firm in which a top executive does maintain a high level of involvement in his firm's MIS. He finds that "the system worked well because each subordinate was keenly aware the president read each . . . computer printout thoroughly and promptly." A significant point here is, as a result, "the data in the printout were regarded as legitimate and meaningful throughout the company."

The need for management involvement and participation in the success of an MIS has caught the attention of many of the writers we have mentioned previously. Another group of authors, including some of the above, investigate the effects of noninvolvement (Avots, 1970; Bieneman, 1972; Churchill, Kempster, & Uretsky, 1969; Kadin & Green, 1971; Kurz, 1973; Hershman, 1968). Churchill et al. find that most organizations isolate the management of their computer resources. Little has been attempted in the application of managerial knowledge and administrative techniques to those relevant areas within the computer system. Bieneman believes that the failure of many computer systems is due, "for all practical purposes," to management's lack of involvement. Avots concurs: computer projects "run into difficulties because of poor specifications and inadequate involvement" on the part of the managers who will ultimately utilize the system. Kadin and Green, and Hershman also think that the failure of an MIS can be attributed to managerial indifference. However, these authors feel that the critical period in which participation is essential occurs during the planning and designing phases. As a result of this lack of participation, managers in effect delegate to the system's experts their control over the MIS project. According to Kadin and Green, control of such a project is essential if MIS failures are to be avoided. Hershman indicates that the noninvolvement of management is due, in part, to the fact that managers "do not even know what information they need to make a decision." Thus when managers begin to criticize the system designers for producing an MIS they cannot use, designers retort with a restatement of management's inability to define its information needs. According to Hershman, the resulting conflict indicates how MIS can influence the "very heart" of an organization: "Thus the battle lines are drawn, and the most likely result is an overflow of useless information."

Poindexter (1969), Powers and Dickson (1973), and Stern (1970) agree that the crux of the MIS problem is not technical; rather, it involves the level and quality of communication between designer and user. Poindexter asserts that systems are designed without incorporating the manager's objectives, that is, that they tend to be created without soliciting managerial input. This seems to suggest that it is not the manager who fails to participate, but rather the designer who fails to solicit external management information. Powers and Dickson indicate that there is a similar lack in the relationship between the user's satisfaction with the system, and the MIS project team who created the system. Stern believes, unlike Poindexter, and Powers and Dickson, that it is not the system's designers who are causing the failures but rather the inabilities and indifferent attitudes of management. Stern states the position that the "greatest barrier" to a successful MIS "is managements' unwillingness to formalize the decision process for periodic decision." Management's unwillingness may be the result of their not knowing what information they actually need and use in decision making, rather than an attitude of noninvolvement in the systems design (Ackoff, 1967).

It would seem that directly related to the level of managerial involvement in an MIS, is the attitude or disposition of those who control the organization's environment. There exists as a result, a range of levels of participation within the organization, which one could identify specific degrees and types of involvement. In accordance, Malcolm and Rowe (1961) suggest that for an effective "integrated management control system . . . a proper point of view on the part of management" is demanded. Taylor and Dean (1966) place empirical labels on the extreme points of the involvement continuum. This range stretches from those organizations where all the executives have been educated in computers, to one organization which had the secretaries retype computer printouts into traditional management report formats. On specific types of attitudes needed, Argyris (1971) asserts that a "climate of rationality" must exist on the part of management if a successful MIS operation is desired. He defines a "climate of rationality" as an unemotional and logical step-by-step approach to the information system and the problems of management. Stern (1970) identifies a managerial attitude that condones participation only under specific circumstances. Management, in this case, assumes the position that a system should not be built unless some segment of management is willing to use it. Stern states that if management purveys this kind of attitude, then MISs will fail. Managers willing to use these systems must be involved in their construction and design.

Holland, Kretlow, & Lignon (1974) have found that 70 percent of MIS systems were "implemented largely as a result of a single individual, or champion, who supported the developing system with his influence, who coordinated the system with the management structure, and who provided the drive necessary to start the system." These findings suggest that a majority of organizations with MISs had them implemented with at least one high-level manager's support, but not—as had been recommended—with the unanimous support of management. Barnett (1969) offers what he calls the "top down format" as another managerial attitude that encourages involvement on a very limited basis. In this "top down format" an executive vice president, second only to the firm's president, controls the MIS and the interaction between system and nonsystem personnel. The level of management involvement is low in the "non-computer executives" and high in those managers who actually use the data. Barnett believes that it is this type of managerial attitude that will more than likely lead to a successful information system.

Another managerial attitude suggested by Murdick and Ross (1972) as a means of promoting involvement and participation in MIS is the cultivating of a very supportive and open environment that stimulates interaction between different departments and individuals within an organization. This type of attitude has also been credited with facilitating managerial participation and involvement in the MIS. Garrity (1963) similarly finds that in cases where "top management fostered a tradition of effective line-staff relations, where top management has created an atmosphere favorable to an innovating, inquiring approach, operating executives have been much more willing to participate" in the MIS effort.

In a study of organizations that utilize MISs, Garrity found that the leading companies had top managers who would specifically state to the rest of management that the organization was committed to the system. Also, these executives would enumerate the specific objectives and the various levels of responsibility needed to achieve stated goals. This implies that a major factor in the success of an MIS is the role of top management. Such involvement is much more important than that of any other level in the management hierarchy. Thus Schoderbek and Babcock (1971) found that the "success of a computer installation is due in no small measure to the degree of leadership and the continuous involvement of top management." And Koontz (1959) and Whisler (1965) pointed to the need for top executives who are actively interested in and fully aware of the impact computer-based systems will have on their organizations. Even more important, top executives must become conscious of the participative roles they must play in the design, implementation, and use of an MIS.

In contrast, Elliott (1974) and Melly (1974) have found few firms where there is little involvement in MIS on the part of the organization's top management. This is regarded as a serious problem by the authors. Attempting to identify the reasons for this lack of involvement, Garrity (1963) and Elliott suggest that top management will interact with the system in proportion to the perceived cost and potential profit from its operation. That is, if top management cannot easily identify the cost/benefit ratio of the MIS, then the likelihood of their participation is extremely low. This behavior is directly related to the quantity and quality of the communications between top management and the systems management. According to Elliott, a communication gap exists, and it is mainly attributable to top management's lack of computer knowledge. Melly expands on this, suggesting that the pace of computer systems development has surpassed the rate at which top management can acquire the requisite knowledge. The "ineffective" nature of "corporate EDP planning" results in little relevancy to the true needs of management, and thus top management is unable to evaluate what it is supposed to control. According to Melly, these top managers "operate in a reactive mode," lacking a specific plan of action. In sum, it appears that the computer system will be inefficiently and ineffectively used by the organization (Murdick & Ross, 1972). Management, as a consequence of this indifference, will be unable to "learn from the past, to pay close attention to the present, and to plan realistically for the future" (Kurz, 1973).

Many of the studies we have noted present interesting conclusions concerning managerial involvement and its impact on MIS. These findings are of two kinds: those that identify the effect of managerial behavior, and those that identify the behavior itself. In the former category are studies done by Coleman and Riley (1972), Churchill, Kempster, and Uretsky (1969), and Murdick and Ross (1972). Churchill et al. have found that when managers remain aloof from the MIS, managerial applications are few, although the MIS was designed and implemented with managerial use in mind. This could be justifiably considered a wasted effort. In the same vein, Murdick and Ross have affirmed that "evidence continues to mount that the results obtained from existing computer-based information systems are something less than expected and that lack of adequate management support heads the list of causes." According to Coleman and Riley, the lack of use, commitment, and involvement by management restricts the impact of MIS on organizations.

Regarding participation and involvement in the MIS, managerial behavior is ambivalent. Schoderbek and Babcock (1971) have found that managers are indeed "taking a more active role in the many areas affecting and affected by the computer." However, Bieneman (1972), Coleman and Riley (1972), Murdick and Ross (1972), and Powers and Dickson (1973), discovered the opposite. They argue that management is no more involved in MIS today than it was in the past. According to Bieneman, managers are tired of hearing that they should be "getting involved." He also finds that "the philosophy of 'preach the need for involvement long enough and it will happen' has not worked," and shows little promise of working in the future. Murdick and Ross demonstrate that the computer technicians, and not management, are the goal setters. Coleman and Riley say that this shift in traditional functions may be the direct result of trying to operate a third generation computer with "first generation users." It would seem that, in this case, the re-education of the MIS user would assist in bringing management up to the sophisticated level of their automated systems. However, if what Bieneman found regarding the lack of managerial involvement were true, then the problem of managerial participation is a dead issue, and methods of circumventing it would need to be studied.

NEED FOR MANAGERIAL TRAINING

"The computer hardware and software is capable of doing almost any job imaginable. The limitations are on the ability of the user to apply computers and not on the abilities of the hardware" (Stern, 1972a). Schewe (1973) states that most of management's attention is centered on the "technical capabilities of the MIS—the hardware and software—while only limited attention is being given to another very important element of management information systems—the system user." As Slater (1967) asserts, this has fostered a "lack of basic EDP understanding by sizable segments of management at all levels." Likewise, Schewe (1973) has found overwhelming inadequacies in the knowledge and skills of the system users he surveyed. Because of these inadequacies, "a gap seems to exist between the desired level of computer competency and the level [actually] existing." In essence, "managers need re-education in the new systems and the new capabilities" (Kleinschrod, 1969).

The very nature of sophisticated computer systems tends to inhibit the easy development of computer-wise managers. The proliferation of hardware and software systems can be mind boggling to the manager. Ultimately, "the success or failure of a concern depends not on the sophistication of the [MIS] but on the training, experience and judgment of the management team" (Burdeau, 1974). According to Bassett (1971): "The ability to use techniques of logic and machine-based systems will be essential for successful job performance."

Hershman (1968) contends that it has somehow escaped people "that an effective MIS must start with an understanding of management rather than with a survey of computers and display devices."

Many authors (Bright, 1963; Churchill, Kempster & Uretsky, 1969; Rowe, 1962; Whisler, 1970b) agree and describe how both the manager and his organization must realize that technological change is reordering management's understanding and needs. The pronounced effect of MISs will be felt with little discrimination on the functions a manager performs. This implies that "all managers must acquire whatever skills and understanding are necessary to work effectively with information technology" (Whisler, 1970b).

Top management has not recognized the interdependency between effective information systems and effective use. Osmond (1971) points out top management's "failure to fully reappraise and understand their own business(es) and particularly the futurity of its operations and interdependence of its various elements." In fact, "many members of top management do not recognize that they are not prepared, managerially, to use computer systems." Thus, he says, "their computer potential remains largely untapped" (Moan, 1973). Whisler (1970a) agrees with Moan, but feels that two factors inhibit the development of effective MISs. One is the slowness in exploiting the potential of equipment, and the second is the "lack of understanding and imagination among higher-level executives, as well as inadequate skills and training." This underutilization due to management's lack of understanding is underscored by Rader (1968). He claims that managers stay aloof from the computer system not only because they lack understanding and support, but also because they realize that changes have to be made throughout the management structure. As Whisler (1965) mentions, managers are going to be displaced or relocated, and either way they will require retraining in the technological skills needed for efficient performance.

Some authors (Holmes, 1970; Vandell, 1970) are more specific about the failings of management. According to Holmes, management personnel have not attempted to educate themselves regarding the computer's ability to produce relevant decision-making data. They are unable to define problem areas clearly, and they do not understand the importance and difficulty of securing accurate input information or the relationship of such input to a successful system. According to Vandell, management's problem-solving behavior in an MIS has two major judgmental requirements. First, the manager must be confident that the technique he is using is the most appropriate one for his particular problem. Second, the means he uses must give him the information he needs for his decision making and for further information processing. But, as Vandell mentions, managers do not now have this ability to recognize the correct procedure or the correct information when they see it. In essence, management does not know how to use the analytical tools or information capacity of their MISs.

The authors we have discussed identify several problems in the educational needs of managers who use computer systems. What we have not discussed is the needs themselves. What will be the computer-created skill requirements of management? Simon (1965) supposes that computerization will stress the need for "systems thinking." Organizations are complex dynamic systems with an assortment of man-machine and machine-machine interactions: thus management education should stress training in servomechanism engineering and/or mathematical functions, since individuals with training in these fields will be more familiar with dynamic systems and will more than likely possess the conceptual tools needed to understand these systems. Bright (1963) anticipates that the need for mathematical competence will increase in the managerial ranks. So do Simon and Melitz (1961). The latter believes that of the many qualities required of a manager, the understanding of mathematical concepts will be one of the most essential. However, managers will not necessarily be required to achieve a particular proficiency in the application of these concepts: familiarity will be more important than skill in application. Melitz identifies several other managerial requirements: "Courage and conviction" will be required as traditional procedures and policies of management are altered. Similarly, Vandell (1970) affirms that "decisiveness" and "courage of the decision maker" are absolute necessities for effective and efficient management. Both authors assert that managers will need to use intuition and imagination in solving ill-structured problems involved with long-term policies and broad objectives. Vandell sees the need for more skill in implementing decisions. He implies that although computer-aided decisions are made, they are not being implemented.

It is of interest to note that Simon (1960a), studying the impact of automation on management, predicts that technical skill requirements will increase only during the early stages of computerization. After this initial period, management's "need to know about the details" of the system will decrease. This longitudinal projection has not been immediately substantiated or discussed by any of the authors reviewed to date, although Melitz (1961) alludes to it when he says that technological knowledge will not be a prerequisite for managers in the future computerized organization. This does not directly address the longitudinal question, but does counter the claims previously noted concerning the skill needs of managers in a computer-based system.

As for the skill requirements and/or the retraining needs of specific levels in the management structure, top executives seem to have received the most coverage. The other studies deal with the knowledge requirements of both middle- and lower-level management.

These studies do not concentrate on either level, but describe generally what may occur with regard to computerization (Baum & Burck, 1969; Ernst, 1970; Taylor & Dean, 1966). Leavitt and Whisler (1958) predict that the emergence of information technology will radically change certain administrative practices of top management. They feel that the training necessary to cope with the increased technology will be taken over more and more by universities. On-the-job training will be used in conjunction with the university, as positions such as "assistant to the senior executive" become educational stations. Reynolds (1969) agrees with both Bright (1963) and Simon (1965) concerning the increased quantitative nature of top management's job. He envisions top executives bewildered by young specialists trained in quantitative methods, and ultimately losing contact with the changes occurring in lower levels of management.

Horton (1974) feels that "top management was often too lazy, too inexperienced or too uninformed to direct the development of organization-wide information management policies." The implication here is that top management needs to be retrained in the quantitative skills required in the changing technological world, and in their participative role in the establishment and maintenance of an MIS for their own survival. This assumes that if top management shies away from interactions with the computer-system specialists, a power shift may occur, and top management may lose most of its controlling or manipulating ability (Field, 1970).

Baum and Burack (1969), however, have studied several firms and found that upper management "was relatively computer literate": three-fifths of the top management level surveyed had some knowledge of computers. This finding seems to contradict the projections of the authors previously noted, although the firms included in Baum's and Burack's study may not be too representative. The study also notes that lower management has a relatively poor understanding of information technology. The authors attribute this wide disparity to the different corporate attitudes among levels in the management structure. Such attitudinal bias is perpetuated in the retraining of supervisory personnel and in the application of computer technology to specific functional areas. The lack of conceptual thought on the part of lower management stems from the limited scope of the corporation's training program.

Taylor and Dean (1966) describe a situation in which a "faith-and-understanding gap" appears between previously trained computer groups and operating managers. The latter are utilizing new methods, but have not been trained in these systems. Consequently, they do not truly understand them. This problem is the result of attempts to force computer applications upon lower managers, who have no education into the nature of the computer system, although they work in functional areas. Ernst (1970) feels that the use of computers will eliminate a basic training ground for future management. He claims that as greater efficiency is gained by automating certain echelons of the organization and ultimately eliminating them, those positions traditionally used to train future managers will be eliminated, too. If this reduction occurred, "staff rather than line positions" would provide the on-the-job training for senior executives of the future. Ernst declares that as computer usage increases, "there will be less and less opportunity to develop junior and intermediate management skills. This must be faced as a real threat."

What can be done to assist in the re-education of management? Stern (1970) says that if the manager were involved in the system's design, creation, and implementation, he should be able to pinpoint those decision areas that need to be attacked, and to identify the information relevant to them. The purpose here is not to burden the manager with unnecessary information concerning the hardware and software of the system, but to orient him to "new ways of thinking about problem solving, evaluation, and control techniques" (Slater, 1967). The manager will be placed in a situation that forces him to acquire more knowledge about the computer and its capacities. In the long term, he will learn how to make his job easier. Taylor and Dean (1966) declare that an "ancillary function of educating management about the computer" may occur in response to computer system auditing. This method, they feel, may be a better means of educating management than any of those normally used. They also note that as auditing procedures and objectives were improved, "more members of management, not directly concerned with the computer effort," were becoming involved. Thus, familiarity with computer techniques and skills spread further into the management structure. Becker (1970) also thinks that the extended use of the computer in training personnel would spread knowledge of computer technology throughout the management structure.

Powers and Dickson (1973) suggest that management's failure to utilize the computer system may be due to a lack of understanding. Computer system design does not encourage managerial input; as a result, most managers have very little basic knowledge concerning the computer system and its uses. The remedy typically incorporates the manager, who will ultimately use the system, into the design and implementation of computerized information systems. Such participation will increase the manager's understanding and thus aid in decision making (Powers & Dickson, 1973). As Holmes (1970) says, a "successful MIS must consider the current and future management information needs." Responding to the assertion that MISs are more a myth than a miracle, and that they have not lived up to their promise,

Schewe (1973) claims that "the fault lies at least in part in the neglect of the system user." If this re-education problem is not reckoned with, "no matter how technically competent an MIS is developed, its true potential will never be realized."

THREAT TO MANAGEMENT

Up to now, we have discussed the actual or potential impact of MIS on managerial practices, numbers, and needs. Nothing, however, has been said about the psychological effects or the behavior resulting from MIS impact on management. As information technology rechannels the organization's flow of information, "managers may come face to face with decisions to inaugurate changes which can substantially influence their own lives" (Whisler & Shultz, 1962). According to Leavitt and Whisler (1958), "perhaps the biggest step managers need to take is an internal, psychological one." The fact is, "information technology will challenge many long-established practices and doctrines, [managers] will need to rethink some attitudes and values which [they] have [long] taken for granted." It is in this environment of change that problems begin to arise. "Those in authority, those accustomed to planning and initiating change, now become the objects of change themselves. The inevitable problems of motivation and morale, of reluctance to change, of feelings of anxiety and threat, will be shouldered by those who are supposed to be doing an effective and rational job of problem-solving and strategy-planning" (Whisler, 1970a). The essential point here is that management feels anxious and threatened by MIS. This leads in turn to other problems.

Stewart (1971) claims that the most common cause of difficulty in MISs is the real or imagined threat of the system to the manager. Several explanations have been offered, all with a common theme: the MIS is considered an agent of change, and, as such, produces anxiety. In fact, MIS will initiate changes in a great many areas, including displacement and/or replacement of managers; loss of security and status; encroachment on traditional decision-making rights of management; increased use of quantitative factors and analysis; increased inter- and intra-departmental communication, resulting in a feeling of over-exposure or higher visibility; lack of knowledge or basic understanding of the system; loss of control; reduced opportunities for advancement; and the possibility that one's incompetence may be exposed by the system (Berkwitt, 1966; Burck, 1964a; Fiock, 1962; Holmes, 1970; Kraut, 1962; Radford, 1973; Stewart, 1971). Argyris (1971) argues that the introduction of a sophisticated MIS represents "a stressful and emotional problem to the participants," and may cause "increasing amounts of psychological failure," measured in fear, alienation, and disenchantment.

Stewart (1971) believes that some managers may dread MISs because they perceive the computer as a "mysterious black box." Such an attitude may have its origin in the manager's lack of basic MIS knowledge, in other words, in plain ignorance. Ackoff (1967) believes this to be the case. He charges that, because MISs are designed in "innocuous and unobtrusive" ways, managers will be unable to appraise them. They will become fearful if they do attempt an evaluation. Their ignorance would become public knowledge, and they would be discredited. Thus another threat is introduced: since the manager is usually not capable of evaluating the MIS, the designers will be delegated much of the control of the organization. For management this loss of control represents an acute threat.

The same is true of increased visibility or exposure due to the inherent processing ability and hardware characteristics of MISs. Fiock (1962) compares the introduction of an MIS to "moving into a glass house." The manager may be intimidated by the computer tape, containing the equivalent of a normal file cabinet: his data can be picked up, read, and misunderstood, and he can be fired without ever knowing why. Although Fiock's scenario may exaggerate, the fact is that formerly inaccessible data can now readily become common knowledge, without any input or control on the part of the manager himself. Radford (1973) thinks that this type of "psychological failure" will be "particularly noticeable in those who are not confident of their position or their ability or who have not established a relationship of trust with their superiors."

Leavitt and Whisler (1958) predicted that information technology will thin the ranks of management. The fear of such a consequence has, perhaps, proved the most powerful of those fears engendered by information technology. Burck (1964a; 1964b) varies the theme slightly. He believes that management's trepidation comes from the realization that their displacement may be a more persistent and difficult problem than the displacement of the blue and white collar employees has been. Although the origin may be different, the cause is the same: fear of losing one's job through displacement or severance.

Alienation, too, has been considered a "psychological failure" attributable to MISs (Berkwitt, 1966; Brill, 1974; Nicholoson, 1963). MIS-created alienation can be either an intra- or inter-individual affect. The first concerns the impact upon the manager within his personal sphere; the second concerns the interaction of managers with other groups in the organization. Berkwitt identifies what he feels is the "most critical period in the life of the . . . manager," the introduction or "phasing-in" of the computer information system.

It is at this point that the manager may experience personal alienation caused by the "starkly new situation in which his years of experience, his painfully acquired know-how, and his personal relationships with top management seem to no longer apply" (Berkwitt, 1966). The previously familiar work environment may become fearfully foreign to him. The stress of personal separation takes its toll on both the individual and the organization.

The other form of alienation created indirectly by the introduction of MISs centers on inter-departmental or inter-group relationships. Brill thinks that the separation of systems analysts from the firm's managers occurs because organizations pool their systems personnel into an "internal consulting activity." As a consequence, the systems function might become so complex that "only members of a new technology priesthood could interpret the wishes of the user into a form that the machine could understand."

Nicholoson identifies another cause of friction, and possibly alienation, between organizational groups: the stress created when two groups attempt to define the problems the system is supposed to address. Nicholoson declares that managers, with a realistic view of their problems, may have difficulty conveying to systems designers, with a theoretical view of problem solving, the processes by which decisions are made—let alone the information necessary for arriving at solutions. The friction created by this difference in viewpoints could foster alienation on the part of either party, depending on whose position was adopted.

Disenchantment may also be a consequence of the introduction and utilization of MISs. Hershman (1968) identifies some of the confusions and mistakes that have contributed to management's disenchantment with MIS. There was the "very real fear of throwing good money after bad." But error and disarray were not the only causes of management's disenchantment, which like alienation, has a multitude of causes, especially in an environment of technological change. The point is, managerial failings must be considered a major factor in the MIS environment.

Consistent with Berkwitt's (1966) notion of "computer-manager impasse," and the concept of "psychological failure" discussed by Argyris (1971), a specific repertoire of behavior can be expected on the part of those individuals who interact with, or utilize, MISs. These actions can be classified into four categories—resistance, shielding, withdrawal, and self orientation. (This scheme is by no means all-inclusive, but it reflects the areas covered in the literature.)

An "often overlooked retarding factor [in introducing MISs] is the human opposition to computerization" (Vergin, 1967). According to Vergin, managers resist information systems because they perceive those systems as a threat to their own positions. Several MIS-related experiences have been discussed as challenges to management and, therefore, causes of resistance. Argyris (1971) describes three experiences that would cause managers to resist MIS: "a reduction of free space" (the restriction of the manager's freedom of movement within his environment); "decreased feelings of essentiality"; and "leadership based on more competence than formal power." The first experience may occur as the system is introduced and the job requirements of the manager are more specific than in the past. Restriction can also occur as routine management operations are taken over by the computer: the result may be a "decreased feeling of essentiality." In fact, if the MIS alters the organizational or management structure, the manager may try to obstruct it. Kraut (1962) thinks that the loss of status or opportunities for advancement will contribute to a reluctance of management to cooperate with the system operators. The loss of status and potential for promotion may very well stimulate a feeling of decreased importance, especially since the perception of essentiality is closely related to a manager's level of participation in the organization's decision-making process. Vergin also suggests that alterations in both the level of participation and the decision-making process itself will make for a less than receptive attitude toward MIS.

The manager's perception of threat will depend, too, on the relationship of competence and power. A competent manager may have little power; an incompetent manager may have a great deal. Both these situations could occur as a result of change from the opposite power position. Under the situational parameter of incompetence, Fiock (1962) affirms that change may be "impeded by the personal fears and ingrained habits of some personnel whose irrational resistance to change stems from the fear that if they admit that improvements in their functions are possible, then they are indicting themselves for having lived so long with inefficiency." According to Radford (1973), "the introduction of an information system requires managers to exercise new skills at a level higher than may have been the case in the past." Also, he says, incompetent employees "can be expected to resist the introduction of any system that might reveal their true or believed incompetence." The alternative profile is one of low morale, low motivation, and probably inefficient production. The implementation of a system that takes full advantage of competent personnel by allowing them to assume appropriate levels of authority will be resisted by those most likely to lose. This will be especially significant if the manager is currently in a position of responsibility. In essence, "those who see their own positions being threatened by a change will be reluctant to adopt it" (Whisler, 1965).

Shielding oneself from other levels or groups of management is another form of behavior attributed to the introduction of an MIS, specifically to the impact of MIS on the communication networks within the organization (Fiock, 1962). This feeling of "exposure" or "high visibility" leads to the fear on the part of top management that their data will be misunderstood since they lack proper input or control. Fiock affirms that "fears like these can lead . . . managers to believe that it is their duty to shield from upper management any knowledge of situations which they could, in time, get straightened out themselves." The failure of computer systems has caused some managers to withdraw by ignoring computer-originated information in lieu of traditional sources (Holmes, 1970). Radford (1973) asserts that withdrawal is a result of the manager's fear of being committed to a well-defined communication network. The problem is that managers may perceive that they have "less room for equivocation in discussions after the initial communication has taken place." Radford also notes that withdrawal is especially noticeable in those managers with little confidence in their position or abilities, and in those "who have not established a relationship of trust with their superiors."

The last type of behavior attributable to the "psychological failure" of management is that of placing one's self-interest above that of other managers and the organization. Whisler (1970a), discussing the impact of technical change, mentions that managers previously able to turn a "deaf ear" to the objections of lower management when changes were planned will now find their "hearing" strongly influenced by their own "self-interest." Decisions concerning the effectiveness and economy of any action may be prejudiced by the "concern over personal welfare." Whisler thinks that this type of behavior may cause the "traditional problems of conflict and suboptimization" to become severe. The consequence will be an inefficiently and organizationally worthless MIS. Moan (1973) identifies a slightly different reason for managerial behavior that inhibits "the effective use of the computer and modern management techniques in most organizations today." He mentions that the relationship of actual to perceived risks will cause management to underutilize the MIS. That is, "even though the risks of not changing outweigh the risks of changing, the fears of the unknown future often outweigh the hazards of the known present." The traditional risk aversion behavior of management may be the real cause of management's perception of MIS as a threat.

Where there is a problem defined, there is usually someone with a solution or remedy. So it is with the threat of MIS to management. Fiock (1962), Horton (1974), and Whisler (1965) each present a means of at least reducing, if not eliminating, the threatening feelings MIS has created within managers. Fiock asserts that the problem can be alleviated through what he calls "proper organization," that is, the placement of both staff and computer operations so that they will be more responsive to the concerns and needs of the functional manager served by the system. Fiock thinks that an environment of "open-mindedness" on the part of top management will assist in reducing managers' fears of high visibility or overexposure. In this kind of atmosphere, the possibility of major misunderstandings would be greatly reduced, and management would not be as fearful of having superiors access their data without their knowledge. Whisler asserts that if managers are to utilize computer technology effectively, they will have to be "objective and deliberate" in their assessment of the impact upon themselves. He also proposes that management be able to "reorganize itself as necessary." Both positions would require a working knowledge of the system's technology. It is here that the basis for an efficient management-system relationship is found. Horton agrees with Whisler that tactful redefinition of both manager and MIS roles is needed. The "coordination approach," that is, simultaneous role definition of manager and MIS, can be used to substantially upgrade MIS's function as a management tool. This approach, according to Horton, has a good chance of success "because it reinforces the functional . . . manager's role and position in the organization, instead of posing a threat to him."

2
EFFECTS OF COMPUTER-BASED MANAGEMENT INFORMATION SYSTEMS UPON THE JOB OF MANAGEMENT

GENERAL FUNCTIONS OF MANAGEMENT

In the beginning, an organization could be directed by a single executive and a few operational managers. Now the organization is stratified and consists of top, middle, and lower management functions. This complexity will grow unreasonable without the assistance of MIS (Hanold, 1968). Hanold argues that the organization will no longer be effective if changes are not made in the structure and tasks of management. The only system "pervasive and responsive enough" to meet the demands of this extremely complex environment is an MIS. Before discussing the literature concerning the impact of MISs upon the job and functions required of management, a brief clarifying statement must be made regarding the function of management. The manager, according to Weber (1959), is that person who, being a member of an organization, is involved in "planning and innovation, coordination, administration and control, and routine supervision of the enterprise." Shaul (1964) defines management in terms of planning, staffing, controlling, and organizing. Although the labels change from author to author, it is generally agreed that these are the functions that make up the manager's job. Not only do such functions incorporate some degree of generality; they also suggest that there is little variation throughout the management structure. Porter and Ghiselli (1957) believe that there are no lucid divisions between the different management strata. This was qualified, however, by reference to management as a "continuum with persons at the highest point being concerned with the very broadest functions and those at the lowest levels being concerned with most specific functions." The functions remain the same throughout the management structure: only the scope or field of view changes. Thus, diverse levels in the structure will have distinct functional requirements for performing the managerial job, and, as a result, will be influenced differently by an MIS.

In the literature, of the three levels in the management structure, only two, top and middle, have received coverage concerning the impact of MIS on their functions and jobs. It may be best, before continuing, to clarify what a top and/or middle manager normally does on the job. As mentioned earlier, the higher one travels in the management structure, the more expanded is one's perspective. Top management personnel attain a global view. They have described themselves as the "dynamic brains of the organization," "action-oriented idea men," the innovators or entrepreneurs of the firm (Porter & Ghiselli, 1957). Dearden (1966) defines top management as those who hold executive vice-presidential and presidential positions in a centralized organization, or those acting as division managers in a decentralized organization. With these positional definitions, Dearden presents his version of the functional requirements of top management. These functions include "management and operating" control, "strategic" planning, coordination, "personnel planning" or staffing, and a new function called "personal appearances." Except for the last, these functions are virtually synonymous with those named earlier. According to Dearden, the performance of this activity is a result of the other five functions. Certain job-related tasks—from business-related entertainment to presentation of service awards to employees—require the personal appearance of the top manager. Dearden assumes that this expected activity will not be affected by MIS, and therefore should not be considered when discussing the impact of MIS on top management. We concur and will follow this format.

As for the middle management ranks, it is defined by Porter and Ghiselli (1957) as the "reality testing mechanism" of the organization. Ideas are filtered down from top management, the "dynamic brains," to middle management, the "reality testers," who determine whether or not these ideas are functional. Middle management personnel view themselves as the "backbone of the organization." They perform the same functions as top management, but their perspective is more narrow and more operationally oriented. They contribute to the stability an organization needs to exist. In essence, middle management "mediates between the top-most layer and all of the other layers of the organization" (Porter & Ghiselli, 1957).

In order to present more clearly the results of our review of the literature, we have divided the material into five subject areas. One is the impact of MIS on the job of management in toto. But the job may also be thought of in terms of the previously mentioned functional requirements. Thus two topic areas are devoted to the implications for both top and middle management: they are specifically concerned with the differential impact between the two strata. This is the basic approach, within which each area will be discussed generally at first, then specifically.

"To play its leadership role effectively, . . . management . . . has required the development of the necessary management tools" (Garrity, 1963). One of these tools is the MIS, in consideration of which Vazsonyi prognosticated in 1954 that "significant changes" would occur in the job of management. After a generation, Vazsonyi (1973a) found that such changes had indeed occurred. In light of these changes, Churchill, Kempster, and Uretsky (1969), Haberstroh (1961), Uris (1963b), Vergin and Grimes (1964), Whisler (1970a), and Walker (1968) all conclude that the content, the functions, and the job characteristics of management will also be affected. That is, as the role changes, so will the tasks required of that role. The MIS and the technological changes produced by it will alter not only the activities and tasks management is responsible for, but also the manager's "personal methods of operation" (Churchill, Kempster, & Uretsky, 1969). Vergin and Grimes find that some managers mention that "the computer had a deteriorative effect" on their job environments. To some executives the transformation is negative and all inclusive. Uris and Whisler think that the contents (all the functions, characteristics, and sub-roles) of the manager's job are changing. Both authors stress the need for upgrading and specialization of the manager's skill level and technical expertise. These conclusions follow closely those discussed in an earlier section concerning the need of management in an MIS environment for re-education and training in computer-based technology.

In reference to Porter and Ghiselli's (1957) statement concerning the scope or viewpoint of specific levels in the management structure, Haberstroh (1961) predicts that managerial activities will no longer be tied to organizational status or position. Haberstroh infers that the functional scope of organizational positions will no longer be management-level oriented. Rather, the continuum of global to specific functions will become task-oriented and will vary within a management level. Besides internal variation, structural levels will continue to display the traditional range of activities described by Porter and Ghiselli. As changes in managerial scope and perspective occur, so will the attitudinal or philosophic requirements of the manager's job (Karp, 1971; Murdick & Ross, 1972; Vandell, 1970). Karp foresees a future when the practical manager will be replaced by an individual with "creative imagination and a broad outlook." This "breed of manager will be a generalist who understands the need to bring the diverse elements of the organization" into the system (Murdick & Ross, 1972). According to Murdick and Ross, the systemic approach to the job of management is a direct result of the introduction and utilization of an MIS. Ancillary to these alterations in the scope of the manager's job is the increased importance of analytical ability. Although Vandell (1970) agrees that analytical skills will be important, he thinks that the art of management will "reestablish its ascendency" as a result of the socialization that takes place when MISs become routinized and the tremendous demand for analytical thought correspondingly decreases.

Technology will alter the patterns of a manager's personal modus operandi (Churchill et al., 1969). Mahoney, Jerdee, and Carroll (1965) claim that the "demands of the physical and technological environment serve as constraints upon managerial behavior, but they are not critical characteristics of managerial jobs." Then what are the characteristics of a manager's job in an MIS environment? Whisler (1970b) attempts to define the characteristics of the task of management in terms of information technology. These characteristics include "goal setting, pattern perception, communication, and computation." Whisler thinks that these characteristics will vary according to the task of the manager. He also believes that information technology will influence the mix of a manager's activities, and perhaps usurp some of the traditional characteristics such as communication and computation. In the realm of communications, Keegan (1974) found that a key attribute of management is not "knowing a great deal of information but of knowing whom to consult." This suggests that managers will alter their communication patterns if they have an MIS that facilitates consultation.

Also in the area of managerial task behavior, several authors (Churchill, Kempster, & Uretsky, 1969; Greenless, 1971) discuss the impact MIS will have, or will not have, on the manager's day-to-day actions. Churchill et al. find that there is variation in the intensity of the relationship between the utilization of an MIS and the conduct of day-to-day managerial tasks. This ranges from "passive" reception of routine data reports to personal interactions with information systems for specific purposes. Greenless sees very little MIS impact on the "day-to-day or operational management" roles. Like Churchill et al., he mentions that "special-purpose" functions will sustain the greatest change as a result of MIS. Routinized managerial activities will not be greatly affected, but the more unique functions will require increasing amounts of computer-based information in order to perform efficiently. McDonough (1966) proposes a new outlook on the relationship between managerial job responsibility and the information system. It is McDonough's position that the MIS should serve the manager. Too often, he feels, the reverse is assumed—that the "manager exists to serve the information system." Obviously, if such an attitude exists in an organization, the efficiency and effectiveness of the manager's role and functions will depend, not on the individual position holder and his abilities, but on the capabilities of the information system. The question is, who should come first: the information system or the manager? McDonough stresses that it should, as a necessity, be the manager.

SPECIFIC TASKS OF MANAGEMENT

In the previous section, five functions of management were described. Traditionally, the number has varied from four to eight (Miner, 1971). The original elaboration of the managerial process or job into functions was done by Henri Fayol in 1916, but not until 1929 were his ideas published in English. Fayol (1929) identified the five activities as planning, organizing, commanding, coordinating, and controlling. Commanding is not as common in today's literature as is the addition of staffing. Although these functions are by no means synonymous or interchangeable, it would seem that the separate function of commanding has been absorbed into the coordination function, while staffing has been added to denominate the task of placing and utilizing personnel. "Planning" includes all those processes that eventually result in a set of future-oriented guidelines for action. "Organizing" includes activities that bring structure to jobs, tasks, or authority. "Coordinating" means directing tasks and subordinates, as well as solidifying individual efforts and directing them toward a specific goal or objective. "Controlling" means insuring that the actual and planned set of actions are consistent.

The management function of planning has received considerable coverage in the literature. Planning may represent the most important set of activities a manager is concerned with, and he spends more time on this function than on others. Rowe (1961) has found that, prior to the introduction of an MIS, management spent 25 percent of its time in the single function of planning. It seems obvious that, if management were to expend its energies equally among the five functions, each would receive only 20 percent of the total time available. Rowe's findings suggest that planning receives a disproportionate amount of management's worktime. Beged-Dov (1967) and Shaul (1964) say that when an MIS is implemented, the time employed in planning increases, compared to current standards. Both authors agree on the cause of this increase. They think that the time spent in search and analysis of information will decrease as the volume and accuracy of planning information increases. As less time is required in the search mode, more time is utilized in the planning function. Consequently, more detailed analysis of alternatives takes place.

Whisler (1965), however, disagrees with Shaul and Beged-Dov. He thinks that computer technology will shorten the time spent in planning and that more frequent and reliable planning information will make easier the adoption of a "new technique and rhythm of planning." He suggests that the utilization of computer simulation techniques will supplement or replace the planning activities of management. Whisler, as well as Burck (1964a; 1964b), believes that the increased availability and utility of new planning tools will give management the ability to investigate and consider more alternatives and contingency plans than time would previously permit. Whisler sees the MIS as a means of extending the time frame of planning into the future, and he considers this beneficial. Dearden (1966) agrees that MISs will appreciably assist in forecasting events, but he foresees no critical need to have these projections continuously updated and immediately available. This suggests that planning, once completed for a specific time frame, need not be altered to reflect the continually changing organizational environment. Apparently, Dearden fails to see any appreciable use for MISs in this function of management.

Organizing, as it relates to the activities of management, has had little if any coverage in the literature. Shaul (1964) seems to be the only author who directly addresses the impact of computer systems on this managerial function. He concludes that "EDP had little effect." Considering the extensive coverage of computer-caused structural changes, one would expect that the literature would be substantial concerning present or projected alterations in the function of organizing—but it is not.

We have suggested that planning is probably the most time-consuming function prior to implementing an MIS. This is challenged, however, by Mahoney, Jerdee, and Carroll (1965), and by Rowe (1961), who have found that, on the average, the most time-consuming function of management is direct supervision of subordinates. Mahoney et al. have determined that 28.4 percent of management's time is spent in coordinating. They have also found that few individual managers resemble the average managerial profile of functional time distribution. "Instead, the typical manager spends a relatively high proportion of his time on a single function" (Mahoney, Jerdee, & Carroll, 1965). Both Rowe and Mahoney et al. imply that the introduction of an MIS will not generally alter the amount of energy expended on this function. Dearden (1966), however, does not expect managers to use MIS at all "in the solution of coordination problems," nor does he anticipate that such a system will have the ability to convey information appropriate to the coordination function. Thus, at least implicitly, these authors agree that managerial coordination activities will not be altered by the organizational use of an MIS.

In direct opposition Melitz (1961) argues that there will be a tremendous increase and upgrading of technically oriented "systems and methods personnel." A coordination problem now arises. Managers will need to know how to deal with technically specialized personnel who are familiar only with laboratory management structures. To Melitz this is an extremely important problem. Berkowitz and Munro (1969) claim that "management is basically the science and art of dealing with and through people," and involves, specifically, the coordinating function. As such, the quality of the MIS, the organization, and management depends upon how good the people are who will ultimately utilize automated management systems. Management needs good staff, but must know how to utilize the system for good coordination. Neel (1971) also believes that MIS will affect management's coordinating activities. He claims that the task of supervising and directing people toward specific objectives will be disrupted by an MIS. The systematizing of information, according to Neel, may lessen an incumbent's job status. This type of change may cause "depersonalization of relationships," "greater distance between people at different levels," and resistance to any introduction of change (Leavitt & Whisler, 1958). All will directly affect the coordination activities of management.

Consideration of the impact of MIS on the control function of management has yielded a variety of findings and opinions, and some disagreement. In a survey of managers, Shaul (1964) has found that with the increase in sophistication and utilization of computer techniques, less time is devoted to control. These managers felt that there would be a decrease in the number of exceptions requiring action, and thus, that less energy would be spent in solving these types of problems. Melitz (1961) agrees that the MIS will facilitate "management by exceptions," in accordance with predescribed criteria. It is Melitz's belief that this computer-assisted technique will eliminate many of the trivial details of controlling, and permit management to spend less time on this function. Taylor and Dean (1966) disagree. They believe, on the contrary, that much more attention will be directed toward this function, because management will be less concerned with the technical complexities of managing and more interested in the overall performance of their responsibilities. Thus, more time will be spent on the organizing and controlling functions. Dearden (1966) indicates that it is possible to utilize MIS in the management control function, although he qualifies this by saying that any attempt to actually use the system "will considerably weaken even a good management control system." Dearden concludes that management control information "cannot be made meaningful—even at an extremely high cost—and that any attempt to do so cannot help but result in a waste of money and management time."

Although staffing is not one of Fayol's original five functions of management, most authors dealing with management jobs tend to include it. In fact, the impact of MIS on this function has been discussed by several writers. Whisler (1965) believes that the amount of time devoted to staffing will increase. He argues that MIS will decrease the "day-to-day firefighting" and ultimately allow the manager to concentrate on development of personnel. Burck (1964a; 1964b) believes that as the computer takes over the routine tasks of management, more and more time will be spent on staffing activities. Shaul (1964) feels that MIS will alter the staffing function by changing the requirements of the positions to be filled. That is, MIS will require a more technically sophisticated individual, and the firm's staffing activities will have to be updated to reflect these new requirements. Jackson (1970) concurs and says that it is more and more difficult and time consuming for management to find the right individuals for the specialized jobs created by MIS. Current jobs are becoming more specialized; this requires management to retrain and re-educate current job holders. Dearden (1966) says that MIS can be of little assistance to management in solving staffing problems. He does, however, see a potential use for MIS in the area of personnel data analysis: the information system can be utilized as a personnel data bank, thus assisting, to some degree, the placement and staffing of qualified individuals. Dearden expects that the impact of MIS on staffing will be thus limited.

Obviously, the literature is full of contradictions concerning the impact of MIS on the performance of management's traditional functions and tasks. But without complete comprehension of just what is being affected in management's tasks, no accurate statement can be made concerning the impact of an MIS on any aspect of management.

ROLES OF TOP MANAGEMENT

We have noted that top managers identify themselves as the "dynamic brains" of the organization (Porter & Ghiselli, 1957). The scope at this level in the management structure is global: top managers are the organization's innovators, change agents, and guiding lights. They are entrepreneurs whose first responsibility is (at least traditionally) to the goals and objectives of the organization. How will the introduction of an MIS affect this level in the management structure?

Leavitt and Whisler (1958), in their classic article, predict that the following changes will occur in top management as a result of information technology: (a) more intense focusing on innovation, change, and "horizon" problems; (b) possible simulation of these processes and ultimate programming of the entire job; (c) more "search-and-research" orientation; (d) less involvement in routine decision making; (e) fading of organizational loyalties in favor of more "rational concerns with difficult problems"; and (f) extreme mobility afforded to experts in particular problems, who are thus free to move from organization to organization. Each of these projected changes implies some degree of expansion in the time devoted to thought processing and less to managerial-type functions. As Anshen (1969) states, top management personnel will be required "to think like philosophers," and he predicts that they will now "stretch their minds beyond the management of physical resources . . . to the management of ideas." It is here that a major problem arises. If (as Anshen, and Leavitt and Whisler, predict) the executive is required to become a manager of ideas, "the threat of obsolescence of managers will pass swiftly from today's conversational shocker to tomorrow's operating reality" (Anshen, 1969).

Paralleling the projections concerning the scope of top management's operating perspective, Diebold (1969) finds that "the level of management and the level of abstraction at which computers make their greatest impact is constantly rising." In fact, he says, "the computer is now tackling the less structured, more abstract, and more important problems which are the real concern of the top levels of management." This seems to confirm Anshen's projections concerning managerial obsolescence. If Diebold's findings are typical, it appears certain that the system will create a critical need for top management re-education, retraining, and/or reassessment in the organization. The MIS will become the "central nervous system" of future organizations.

Outside the scope of its role, what potential or actual changes may occur in top management's job function? Vandell (1970) feels that the function of coordinating lower level decision makers will become more time constrained. MIS will reduce time scales, thus creating more intense and diversified pressures on both top and lower management. Contrary to some of the previous authors, Vandell believes that top management, as a result of these pressures, will become heavily involved in "day-to-day control activities in addition to [the] function of leading and developing men" or coordinating. Vandell expects the controlling and coordinating functions to become more difficult, not only because of shortened time frames and heightened pressures, but also because of the "rapidly shifting loci of challenge to which [managers] must respond." Problems will not come consistently from the same source or area within the organization; major changes in top management's function will be required to surmount them.

Burck (1964a; 1964b), Leavitt and Whisler (1958), and Sanders (1969) project that MIS will, in fact, tend to centralize management structure. This centralization will also cluster management functions by facilitating the decision-making process through circumvention of subordinate data inputs, and by allowing top management to process directly from the system. Authority and control will be maintained by top management, and the lower portion of the management structure will be reorganized in order to flatten it more effectively. The complexity of rapidly shifting challenges will be reduced considerably as the structure of the organization becomes more compact. Thus, top management will be able to retain most of its decision-making power and mobility, enabling it to react quickly to unique problem situations without the time delay of subordinate data input.

Jackson (1970) has surveyed several organizations with respect to the impact of computerized information systems on management roles and tasks. "Four of the five top executives indicated that they were able to delegate" control and coordination over short-term organizational objectives to middle management. Thus, Sanders, as well as Leavitt and Whisler, are incorrect in their prediction that MIS will cause recentralization. In fact, Jackson has found that for top management the specialization requirements of their jobs have decreased, so that they can now rely on middle managers to "interpret, analyze, and then relate necessary details to the appropriate executive." Regarding the skill requirements of the job of top management, Jackson's study finds a split of two to three over the impact of the computer. That is, three top managers say that there has been no increase in the functional skill requirements of their jobs, and two say that there has been. In accordance with the three top executives who indicate "no noticeable effect," Gilman (1966) suggests that there will not be a "substantial change to the role of top management," only a more effective and efficient discharge of their traditional responsibilities. Gilman concludes that "the real danger is not that top management will not change their roles to fit the computer, but that they may."

ROLES OF MIDDLE MANAGEMENT

Leavitt and Whisler (1958) predict that the changes in the job of middle management due to information technology would be "reminiscent of (but faster than) the transition from shoemaker to stitcher, from old-time craftsman to today's hourly worker." In other words, the middle manager's work will become highly structured and may be reduced in status (Hoos, 1960; Leavitt & Whisler, 1958). The traditional function of translating broad policies and plans into specific procedures will become increasingly specialized (Porter & Ghiselli, 1957; Uris, 1963b). Burck (1964a; 1964b) agrees that the job of the middle manager will become "more specialized," as well as "highly programmed" and specific. These authors infer that the scope of middle management's task will be truncated with the use of MIS, that is, that specialization will reduce the number of activities and responsibilities of middle managers—and the number of middle managers, as well. Shaul (1964) disagrees: he finds that, "far from contracting the scope of the middle manager's job, [MIS] is expanding it." As more and more activities are assigned to middle management, the job grows more complex. The result will be "faster reaction" for coordinating and controlling, as well as more "elaborate planning." Shaul has also established that, contrary to the prediction that major reductions in the number of middle managers would occur because of increased centralization, MIS has actually increased their numbers, in one case by over 50. Hanold (1968) agrees that there is a trend toward increasing both the "analytical and executive functions" of middle managers. "This latter fact has not been sufficiently described, and no attempt has been made to measure the rate at which this trend is continuing"; neither has there been speculation "respecting the future effect of this phenomenon upon the [organization] and its management."

Uris (1963b), although not exactly agreeing with Shaul and Hanold, has found that "extrapolation of current experience suggests that rather than replacing large numbers of managers, computers will have their major impact on the content of the middle management job." Schwitter (1965), however, finds that although middle management's job content does change, the extent of this change is slight. According to Schwitter, the effect of MIS on the job content of middle management is "minor and slow." If MIS does in fact alter the content of the middle manager's job, what sort of changes may be expected? Schwitter sees potential change as dichotomous. There will be either a qualitative or a quantitative change. (The increasing or decreasing of middle management job responsibility, complexity, and/or training is considered qualitative. Quantitative alterations involve increases or decreases in the function or duties of middle managers, and/or an increase or decrease in the number of subordinates under the manager's control.) Anshen (1960) asserts that MIS will not alter, in any negative sense, the content or number of middle manager tasks. Rather, middle management job content will expand, as will their activities, into areas not given much attention in the past. The tasks middle managers perform will begin to resemble those associated with top management.

Several authors (Greenless, 1971; Jackson, 1970; Sanders, 1969) have identified specific variances in the middle manager's job and its content, due to MIS. In Jackson's study, all of the middle managers surveyed felt that skill levels required to perform their jobs had substantially increased. This, they thought, was due to their increased interaction with the computer system, which involved review of external as well as internal reports, coordination of "several operations with the computer," and direct communication with it (Jackson, 1970). Greenless agrees with Leavitt and Whisler that middle management will be affected more than any other level by MIS implementation. He expects the job content of middle managers to change in order to allow more time for coordinating and planning. Thus middle managers "will be less occupied with ordinary 'brush-fire' management." If this is so, Melitz's (1961) prediction that management-by-exception would become the rule for controlling with MIS has not yet become a reality.

Sanders (1969), discussing the impact of MIS on middle management, identifies three attitudes: conviction that the job will become more rewarding and challenging, pessimism, and a sort of middle-of-the-road feeling that is mostly a function of uncertainty. Pessimists fear that middle management's functions will become less challenging, more routine, repetitive, and highly structured. Also, according to Sanders, pessimists proclaim that many planning, centralizing, coordinating, and staffing decisions will be usurped by the system. The optimists, however, typically counter with predictions of increases in job challenge, control activities, planning tasks, company communications, and organizational coordination. Optimists also see an overall shift toward a position that more closely resembles the top managerial functions. Yet Sanders does not back up either extreme position with facts or findings, nor does he come to any sort of conclusion.

We will discuss separately the five functions of management already mentioned, and consider the actual or projected impact of MIS on these activities. Planning, according to Leavitt and Whisler (1958) and Uris (1963b) will be moved upward in the management structure. MIS will force middle management to relinquish this function to a group of operational research specialists. Coleman and Riley (1972), Ignizio and Shannon (1971), and Jackson (1970) all agree that, with the introduction of MIS, planning will require more involvement and time. Except for Coleman's and Riley's assertions, the evaluation of MIS's impact on middle management planning activities is based on survey findings. Surveying middle management for the impact of MIS on the controlling function, Ignizio and Shannon, as well as Jackson, have found that managers decreased the amount of time and energy expended in these efforts, but that there was an increase in their levels of responsibility. The inference here is that middle managers will delegate routinized controlling activities to subordinates and/or the system, while increasing the number of activities they are controlling.

The managerial function that elicits the most complete coverage in the literature is coordinating or directing. Vergin (1967) has surveyed "middle managers whose positions were most affected by the computer." These managers claim that the system has its most severe impact on the tasks of motivating and coordinating subordinates. Since many of the tasks of middle management are being computerized, there is a substantial reduction in the number of subordinates managed. In addition, the MIS causes many of the remaining employees to feel that they have been downgraded; this in turn creates motivational and coordinational problems. Ultimately, there is a reduction in the time and energy spent on the function of coordinating. Ignizio and Shannon (1971) and Karp (1971) believe that middle managers will increase their coordinating activities as a result of MIS. In fact, Karp claims that the middle manager, relieved of some time-consuming tasks, will "divert his energies into more creative human relationships." Ignizio and Shannon have found that a reduction in the time spent controlling, planning, staffing, and organizing leaves more time for coordinating activities such as motivating and leading. Jackson (1970) is the only author whose findings do not indicate any change in this regulating function. In fact, the middle managers surveyed do not spend any more or less time than usual in coordination activities.

The only functions not covered so far are organizing and staffing. None of the surveys discussed here indicates a change in this function as a result of MIS implementation. It can be inferred, therefore, either that MIS has no impact on organizing, or that the effect is so slight as not to be apparent. Unfortunately, this must be left completely to conjecture. As far as staffing is concerned, Ignizio and Shannon (1971) have found that middle managers do spend more energy on this function. Jackson (1970), however, claims that those managers surveyed had not altered their activities one way or the other, but had increased the time spent on retraining actions. This training time would be either for employees currently holding an organizational position, or for new employees needing to be socialized into the system.

These are the projected and actual effects found in the literature relevant to middle management jobs, roles, tasks, and functions. To reiterate, only four or five studies have been reported in the literature concerning the impact of MIS on these dimensions. Such lack of data indicates that further investigation should be conducted before any consideration of MIS-related effects are assumed to influence additional aspects of managerial behavior.

ALLEGED NULL EFFECTS ON THE JOB OF MANAGEMENT

The 1950s brought the world the information technology explosion. With it came the soothsayers enthusiastically forecasting a "management revolution." They predicted that the computer would drastically alter the manager's organizational life and status. In the middle to late 1960s and early 1970s, a new group of investigators with adamant—and opposite—opinions concluded that management would remain in control and retain its power. This group began to question all of the past, present, and future influences of MIS on management. A few empirical studies of the impact sustained by management were conducted. The conclusions differed markedly from earlier ones. In fact, a great many authors have concluded that the computer and MIS have not affected management as expected (Ackoff, 1967; Alexander, 1969; Brady, 1967; Burck, 1964a; Coleman & Riley, 1972; Dearden, 1967; Ein-Dor, 1975; Jones, 1970; Lee, 1965; Murdick, 1972; Shaul, 1964; Stern, 1972a; Vandell, 1970; Whisler, 1965; et al.).

When the computer was first introduced as the ultimate in management tools, predictions abounded concerning new worlds to be opened up by management's "fair-haired, problem-solving wonder boy." However, the many forecasts of "savings in time, cost, and labor were, and still are, often unrealistic. . . . As a result, disappointments, frustrations, and cynicism developed in some areas, and the computer has now become management's whipping boy" (Megginson, 1963). The promises that MIS held for many managers have gone unfulfilled. These managers thought that, because of MIS's shortcomings, they would continue to manage as they had done previously. To their discomfort and disenchantment, they find that the models and techniques offered by the systems people do not typically fit the manager's needs. Although there has been an improvement in the quality and quantity of information these managers are using, the improvement has not been too dramatic (Stern, 1972a). All in all, it seems that the MISs that have been implemented are not necessarily performing the functions they were designed to exercise.

Of a more specific nature is the literature concerning easily identifiable effects of information technology. Leavitt and Whisler

(1958) predict that the ranks of middle management will be substantially reduced, and the tasks they perform will become routinized and specialized. Lee (1965) is one of the first to study whether or not drastic changes have indeed occurred as a result of computer technology. He finds that there have not been any severe reductions in the numbers of middle managers employed in the organizations studied. Similarly, an editorial ("Computers and middle management," 1966) mentions that a survey conducted by the American Foundation on Automation and Employment has found that "the spectre of widespread, computer-caused unemployment among middle managers is still only a ghost story." However, the editorial qualifies this by crediting the economic boom of this period with absorbing those middle managers who were removed. The implication is that computer-based systems are displacing middle managers, but that the overall effect is not as catastrophic as predicted.

Coleman and Riley (1972) affirm, however, like Lee (1965), that no research up to that time has "documented causal or contributory relationships between MIS and the elimination of middle managers." These authors attribute this lack of impact, not to the economy, but to the tremendous variability of operational-type problems, plans, and decisions. Middle managers have to perform a broad range of tasks that have little programmed information: MIS can complement their efforts, but not easily eliminate them. The degree of routinization and specialization of the middle manager's job has also received fair coverage. As mentioned earlier, Leavitt and Whisler (1958) first predict that information technology will automate middle management positions. After reconsidering the evidence, Whisler (1965) concludes that the first prediction was unfounded and cannot be supported further. Other studies (Burck, 1964a, 1964b; Schwitter, 1965; Shaul, 1964) affirm this lack of impact. Shaul also finds that the projected demise of the middle manager's status because of routinization and specialization in job content has not occurred. In light of what little data there is, it is not surprising that other prognostications have proved wrong.

Several other authors ("Computers and middle management," 1966; Dale, 1964; Parsons, 1968; Shaul, 1964) also discuss the lack of MIS impact on the job content and functions of middle management. Of these authors, both Dale and Shaul claim that no evidence exists to indicate that middle management's job or position have been affected by the introduction and use of MIS. Parsons contends that, although MIS may be altering many areas in the organization, it is not changing management functions such as planning, organizing, controlling, coordinating, and staffing. In Parsons' view, the system is nothing more than a management tool, and, as such, should only affect management insofar as it facilitates basic management functions.

The top level in the management hierarchy has not been influenced as drastically as was originally thought by many writers ("A new look," 1965; Sanders, 1969; Stewart, 1971). In fact, top management has not been directly benefited or changed by the MIS, though it has received some "sizable headaches" during installation ("A new look," 1965). Sanders perceives that MIS can remove some of the uncertainty associated with the unique and ill-structured problems of top management. He does not consider that this assistance from MIS will substantially change top management's role. Stewart summarizes the situation when he says that "little use has been made of the potentiality of the computer" and thus there has been "little impact on management, especially top management." Similarly, Coleman and Riley (1972) suggest that "top managers have not changed significantly their planning techniques, types of plans made, nor their decision-making approaches." And Brady (1967) and Kanter (1972), surveying several organizations' top managers, find "no instance of direct use of the computer by top management for decision making." In fact, these top managers do not receive, directly, any kind of computer-generated information. Brady and Kanter conclude that "if the computer has had any impact on the top management decision-making process in the companies studied, the effect has not been directly on top management, but on the manner in which middle managers are contributing to top management decision making." That is to say, the middle manager will process the computer-generated information before it is allowed to rise to the level of its ultimate use. This could mean that daily decisions will be handled routinely by middle managers, and not be usurped by the computer (Alexander, 1969).

Attempting to identify why top managers and their decision-making processes have not been affected as predicted, several authors (Alexander, 1969; Churchill, Kempster, & Uretsky, 1969; Stewart, 1971) claim that the unstructured, open-ended nature of their activities resist quantification, and, therefore, are not programmable. In fact, Alexander affirms that "management is less amenable to computerization than was formerly believed." Not only are top managerial decisions and tasks generalized and unstructured: top managers spend more than half of their time in selecting and motivating their personnel. Such a task is not readily computerized.

In light of these findings showing the very slight impact of MIS, a group of authors (Ackoff, 1967; Jones, 1970; Murdick, 1972; Schoderbek, 1971; Stewart, 1971; Vandell, 1970) attempt to identify the causes. Schoderbek states that, according to some, the failure of MIS to live up to expectations is attributable to management, and not to "any inherent defects or shortcomings of the hardware." One of management's failures is the underutilization of the system. According to Ackoff, "contrary to the impression produced by the growing literature, few computerized MISs have been put into operation." Ackoff also finds that if the systems are implemented at all, most will not meet their installer's high expectations. Similarly, Stewart (1971) concludes that the underutilization of MIS is due to "managerial inertia; if this could be overcome the computer would have a great impact on management."

Vandell (1970) identifies several other possible explanations for MIS's failure to influence management. Some of these are (a) the shortage of qualified users; (b) lack of education in computer applications; (c) scarcity of ready-made programs for decision making; and (d) lack of top management's involvement in the system. Along these same lines, Murdick (1972) mentions that the lack of impact has been slow, because of "inadequate staff, lack of managerial involvement, and the economics of adapting to a new technology." The whole problem, as Schoderbek has said, is not with the new technology or hardware, but with "brainware." Management, not the systems analyst, has the talent to design and program an effective, efficient, and viable MIS. This problem has been augmented by the assumption that the computer will employ the manager—not the manager the computer. In addition, those who design MISs have tended to concentrate on "gimmickry," rather than factors important to the manager in performing his role (Murdick, 1972).

Despite all the literature, Jones (1970) still forecasts "far-reaching changes in decision making in the years ahead." These changes will result, not from the computer itself, but from managers interacting with computers. With regard to all those writers who have projected and/or found that MIS did have an impact upon management, and those who failed to predict or verify the projected changes, Ein-Dor (1975) concludes that "the only ground for general agreement is that the performance of MIS (however defined) has been disappointing to date, and that the hopes placed in such systems have not been realized."

3
IMPACT OF COMPUTER-BASED MANAGEMENT INFORMATION SYSTEMS UPON MANAGERIAL DECISION MAKING

DEFINITION OF MANAGEMENT DECISION SYSTEM

Due to its embryonic state, the definition of a "management information decision system" is not yet stable. Apparently, further refinement and specification of the nature of this system are needed. Functionally speaking, Dickson (1968) declares that a management decision system (MDS) "is a blend of organizational theory, accounting statistics, mathematical modeling, and econometrics, together with exposure in depth to advanced computer hardware and software systems." Wynne and Dickson (1975) specify the essential elements of an MDS as men and computers collaborating interactively, each playing for the other a complementary role. Normally, insight and judgment are provided by personnel, while storage, retrieval, and processing operations are the work of computers. This man-machine symbiosis is constrained by the continuously updated data that reflect the status of the internal and/or external organizational environment.

It should be stressed that the joint utilization of information by this man-machine system is highly decision-oriented. That is, this system embodies by design the decision cycle to provide action alternatives, probable payoffs, preferred implementation, rapid feedback, and continuous monitoring. Garrity (1971) states that the aim of these decision systems is "to develop an effective blend of human intelligence, information, technology, and management science, which interact closely to solve complex problems." Sprague and Watson (1975a) assert that the essential elements of a "decision support system" are the decision maker, derived data, and mathematical models. It is paramount that these MDSs concentrate on the actual process of making decisions, and not isolate inputs that are integral to the process. Precise procedures are presented to a person to aid him in decision making. Typically, a decision technique is linked directly to an information source; that is, it is an integrated decision system. According to Dickson (1968), a "true information system" not only embraces information that is relevant to decision making, but also displays it at the proper moment in a meaningful format.

DESIGN AND DEVELOPMENT OF MANAGEMENT DECISION SYSTEMS

One way to make the best use of the manager's time is to design and develop an MDS to support him. In order to accomplish these tasks it is important, first, to analyze what critical decisions have to be made; second, to establish efficient and effective strategies for making them; and third, to design a system that merges the decision maker, the mathematical models, the data bases and the computational power of a mainframe. It must be emphasized that an MDS is not merely an amalgamation of hardware and software: rather, it is an abstraction made real by advances in technology. Morton (1971) mentions that "failure to do a decent job of analysis may result in solving the wrong problem or designing an inappropriate system for problem solution."

Typically, MISs have been designed to generate data and reports for traditional business functions. Reams of these computer-based data are planned to support everyday operations of the organization. "Rarely are they deliberately designed to support significant <u>managerial</u> decisions" (Morton, 1971). Simon (1967) says that the trend toward automating operational decisions will alter managerial responsibilities by concentrating them more on developing automated decision rules and policies, and attempting to better the decision process and system. The concept of "management by expectation" will probably be replaced by "management by the design of decision systems" (Simon, 1967). Appropriate MDS design procedure is of paramount importance in implementing this change. The initial step demands that the managerial decision structure be analyzed to determine the types of decisions that are made, and the interrelationships among them. Through decision-flow analysis, salient decisions that are made by default can be identified, together with interrelated decisions that are made independently (Ackoff, 1967).

Rowe (1961) affirms that many facets of decision making should be considered when designing an MDS:

1. The bases or criteria for making decisions.
2. The information required to make decisions.
3. Where decisions are made and by whom.

4. The number and type of decisions made at various organizational levels.
5. The response rate required for decisions after information is received.
6. The time taken to actually make the decisions.
7. The induced lags or delays in information flow due to decision making.
8. The noise or errors in the decision-making process.
9. The relation of organizational structure to decision making.
10. The bases for automating decisions. (p. 68)

Having access to these decision dynamics and structures, the MDS designer should be able to understand more fully the nature of the problem-solving process. Thus, he should be able to improve decision making by creating a system based on his increased knowledge of the implicit judgmental models and policies intrinsic to the decision process (Morton, 1971). Stewart, West, Hammond, and Kreith (1975) point out that, in order to be effective, the judgmental aid itself must "externalize the judgment process." Not only does this visibility minimize the guesswork about the nature of the decision-making process to be aided by an MDS; it also usually culminates in objective weighting schemes, utility functions, combinational rules, and consistent judgments.

In order for experts to design and develop MDSs, "the various activities, flows, responses, and behavioral characteristics" of the organizational system must be specified (Rowe, 1962). Information about the states of these subsystems can readily be programmed for display on graphic terminals. Other potential inputs for display include subsystem constraints, algorithms, decision rules, and environmental parameters. If MDSs are not related to the real-time aspects of organizational subsystems, then in most instances they become irrelevant to the manager's needs. This being the case, it becomes extremely difficult, if not impossible, to perfect MDSs with the ability to minimize managerial intervention to the point of complete exclusion—a state of truly automated decision making. If designers of MDSs would rather keep the decision maker "in the loop," then it is highly probable that a manager's inner sanctum will probably take on the aura of a "war room," with its many on-line, graphic terminals linked to one or more mainframes (Krauss, 1970). By setting up an MDS in this manner, a significant benefit can be realized: "incorporation of the computer into decision systems makes possible continuous and rapid feedback of information from the environment to decision points" (Whisler & Shultz, 1960). Managers and their staffs are notorious for their neglect—despite often-repeated advice—to design and develop decision systems following some set of rigorously analytical procedures, such as those mentioned above (Ensign, 1974).

DYNAMICS OF MANAGERIAL DECISIONS

According to Radford (1973), the "climate of rationality" suggests an increased dependence in decision making on quantitative dimensions and explicit processes. Increased emphasis is placed on objective and logical solutions to pertinent problems. An attitude of this sort leaves very little opportunity for subjectivity and irrationality. With minimal ambiguity and fluidity, there is maximal probability that managers will be charged with incompetence if their now visible decisions are not successful (Argyris, 1971). With the current increased trend toward MDS implementation, managerial decision making is not only becoming more analytical and scientific, but is also relying less on intuition and guesswork (Uris, 1963).

Typically, within any MDS there are two classes of decisions—those relating to measurable physical phenomena, and those relating to intangible human values. It is very difficult to assess what information requirements are necessary or sufficient for supporting or aiding these subjective and multidimensional utilities (Burlingame, 1961). Hoos (1960) implies that MDS is antiquating intuitive decision making by emphasizing more objective and overt criteria. However, it is very unlikely that MDSs can be programmed to mimic many of the complex decisions required by management, since there are numerous intangibles and unspecifiable relationships to analyze appropriately and objectively (Uris, 1963b). Koontz (1959) partly supports this view by asserting that many parameters and variables inherent to managerial problems cannot be quantified. Similarly, it seems that managers make no rational or objective decisions at all. According to Vazsonyi (1974), "the chief ingredients in high policy are gut feeling and ethical hunch."

One way to incorporate a decision within a computerized system is to simplify the judgmental process (Vergin, 1967). This usually precludes qualitative factors within the MDS, since these dimensions are definitely difficult to quantify. Thus, it is almost impossible to automate the comprehensive sphere of decision making, subjective as well as objective (Burdeau, 1974). This kind of arduousness may have led Murdick (1972) to exclaim: "Render unto the machine the things that are the machine's and unto man the things that are man's . . . the things of the spirit, the personality, and leadership, which no machine can do." Stern (1972a) even suggests that since the problem solving process is not usually specifiable, it cannot easily be assisted by a computerized process. Managers, as problem solvers, are not confined to only a few action alternatives. Jones (1970) claims that "no computer programs have yet been written which pick from an open-ended range of possible solutions, it is now impossible to arrive at 'managerial' decisions by automatic process." Likewise, Dreyfus (1965) declares that digital computers cannot imitate such essential aspects of human intelligence as "fringe consciousness" (an awareness of environmental stimuli that are simply too numerous to be perceived distinctly), "essence-accident discrimination" (an ability to distinguish indispensable from incidental aspects), and "ambiguity tolerance" (an aptitude for handling situations that are specified precisely). These salient attributes are of course intrinsic to managerial decision making. In light of these shortcomings, it is no surprise to Jones (1970) that "the current trend is away from, not toward, attempts to computerize management decision making. . . . A predetermined single mathematical statement to be minimized or maximized by a mathematical procedure inside a computer has, so far, turned out to be a very poor substitute for the shifting sensitivity of a good business executive."

On the other hand, Yntema and Torgerson (1961) point out that a computer can readily mimic a decision maker's judgmental processes. In fact, they say, these artificially intelligent judgments are, in a few cases, better than those exercised by the decision maker himself. These "humanoid problem-solving techniques"—not algorithmic methods—can handle via "heuristic programs" numerous ill-structured managerial decisions (Simon, 1960c). Kanter (1972) claims, however, that the higher a manager is in the organizational hierarchy, the likelier it is that he never has sufficient information on which to base his decisions. Consequently, the decision maker must resort to his "precognitive ability," that is, instinct, or intuition, which is almost impossible to capture in a heuristic program. Melitz (1961) even implies that many of these decision programs cannot replace the need for managerial judgments.

Alexander (1969) asserts that there is substantial evidence that managerial decision making is an art, not a science. Because it is a less objective or quantitative process, indubitable or absolute answers are likely to be rare. Consequently, managers complain incessantly that "computer solutions" are completely inadequate for their specific decision-making situations. These programmed algorithms are apparently based on too many limiting assumptions and constraining conditions (Kegerreis, 1971). Anshen (1969) says that there are several difficulties in reducing all decision data to a numerically manipulatable set—and serious doubts about whether it can be done at all. Even if it were possible, the dynamics of the decision-making process—the flexibility and adaptability intrinsic to judgment—would probably be excluded. According to Whisler and Shultz (1960), there is a danger that once a decision system is designed and developed, it will be employed in a mechanical way without systematic examination. This is in addition to the predicament created by the overemphasis in MDSs on what is explicit, objective, measurable, and quantitative, to the exclusion of the implicit, subjective, immeasurable, and qualitative.

NATURE OF PROGRAMMED DECISION MAKING

MDSs can be designed so that "decision discretion" is an essential aspect of the automated system. The human component is no longer in the loop once the system is developed, so the decisions themselves are made without the manager's judgment. This kind of system is designed for "programmed" decision making (Dickson, 1968). According to Ansoff (1965), there are several advantages to these totally programmed decision systems. First, a computer can, intrinsically, make these programmed decisions much better than man. Second, an automated decision system frees a manager to handle "nonprogrammed" decisions. Third, a programmed system by nature accelerates decision reaction time, thus improving organizational efficiency. These benefits arise primarily from the ability to specify mathematically functional relationships among quantitative variables, and to state unambiguously judgmental rules and policies.

Karp (1971) implies that by 1980 MDSs will have replaced decision makers in the exercise of programmed decisions dealing with structured situations. However, some individuals ("An overview," 1969) firmly hold the belief that many of the forecasts that proclaimed the programming of structured as well as unstructured decisions are not being realized very rapidly. Much of the difficulty is due primarily to the unstructured, inexact, and impending nature of the data demanded by managerial decisions. It is irksome to attempt to "acquire, update and process" this nebulous information (Kanter, 1972). Consequently, very few MDSs have been developed to handle these perplexing circumstances. Morton (1971) mentions, too, that not only are some managerial problems unstructured or unknown, but that they are also continuously changing. Once a problem is identified, it will probably change by the time an MDS is developed to solve it. In most instances, however, the problem is completely unknown, poorly defined, or lacking in structure. It would indeed be troublesome to try and solve these kinds of problems by a set of programmed decision algorithms. Likewise, a "one-shot decision" can neither be programmed nor solved by an MDS (Stern, 1970).

In some situations MDSs can be constructed to process reams of data and to make many decisions; yet they are still not truly "intelligent." They are incapable of making any sort of generalizable judgment, which a human can (Yntema & Torgerson, 1961). According to some (Simon, 1960c), "computers are just very speedy morons for carrying out arithmetic calculations. . . . They only do what you program them to do." MDSs may make programmed decisions to replace a manager, but they are not likely to mimic him. These systems are just too rigid: they lack the flexibility of the human decision maker to consider new variables or relationships (Vergin, 1967). Anshen (1960) also doubts that many managerial decisions are amenable to programmed decision making. They are just too complex and diversified.

Employing an MDS means utilizing quantitative decision-making techniques. By incorporating these discretionary routines in an automated system, managerial decision makers should have more time to solve those important human relations problems (Whisler & Shultz, 1962). Also, if MDSs are designed with intrinsic decision-making capabilities, managers will be liberated from having to exercise discretionary authority over real-time operational systems (Argyris, 1971; Beckett, 1965). This automated decision-making ability should easily effectuate "management by exception" (Ansoff, 1965). When managerial judgmental policy needs changing, the appropriate programmed decision rule can be modified to reflect this discretionary alteration. The MDS can then be modified to reflect this discretionary alteration. The MDS can then continue to monitor routine operational systems. If the MDS were baffled by some specific circumstance, the manager could easily usurp control from the computer in this exceptional case. It seems that an irreducible number of irregular and critical decisions will still have to be made by management (Uris, 1963b). Regardless of the views of some scientists (Slovic, Fleissner, & Bauman, 1972), certain cognitive choices cannot be simulated by a computer. Apparently, this "growing disillusionment with the capacity of computers to make decisions for managers" has not entirely negated other sundry uses (Jones, 1970). Simon (1960a) says that as managerial decision making becomes more automated, there will be fewer opportunities for "creative drives to be satisfied by exercising discretionary capability." It seems that this price must be paid for producing not only surer management decisions (Kleinschrod, 1969), but also unambiguous policy interpretations (Melitz, 1961). However worthwhile automated decision making may be to a manager, he should not expect a computer to usurp his discretionary ability (Stern, 1972a), nor should he follow its dictates unquestioningly (Kunreuther, 1969).

RELATIONSHIP OF MIDDLE MANAGEMENT AND AUTOMATED DECISION MAKING

A center of controversy has been the capacity of computers to mimic man's cognitive activities, especially decision making (Brabb & Hutchins, 1963). Simon (1960a) asserts confidently that "machines [computers] will be able to perform any function in the organization—and this includes the 'thinking' and 'deciding' tasks that are the basis of the manager's job. . . . [T]he business organization in 1985 will be a highly automated man-machine system, and the nature of management will naturally be conditioned by the nature of the system being managed." Berkwitt (1966) thinks that at least 80 percent of middle management's judgments will ultimately be computerized. He claims that, in a number of operational situations, a computer-based system could make decisions more precisely, quickly, and regularly than most managers. Consequently, the computer has abrogated at least a few routine decisions that were typically exercised by middle management (Vergin, 1967). Burlingame (1961) seems to agree with Hoos' (1960) notion that many middle managers will be eliminated. The trend toward organizational decentralization caused by advances in information technology has reversed. Burlingame mentions that MDSs can not only make better and more rapid decisions than middle managers; they can also structure information flow so that decentralized discretionary responsibility is minimized. It seems that only the "top-level managerial elite" will actually exercise unautomated decision making. Consequently, many middle managers will have to derive personal satisfaction, which had been previously obtained from problem solving and decision making, from off-job activities.

Several authors (Lee, 1967; Simon, 1960c; Uris, 1963b) have proclaimed that decisions that have typically been made by middle managers will now be made by computers. Thus, they do not hesitate to assert that many middle managers are extremely vulnerable to replacement by computerized systems, which may ultimately lead to a much smaller number of these executives in existing enterprises. Encroachment on the "decision-maker's domain" by automated decision systems will also lead to an "impersonalistic" discretionary process (Whisler & Shultz, 1960; Eilon, 1969). Such a system simply and mechanistically outputs whatever increasingly contingent decision algorithms have been programmed into it. Consequently, the managerial decision maker becomes increasingly superfluous. When decision discretion is "completely impersonalistic, the decision-maker ceases to have a meaningful role; he ceases to be a decision-maker" (Eilon, 1969). Managerial mystique often attributed to "judgment," "experience," and "creativity" (Simon,

1967) cannot possibly withstand the inevitable intrusion of factual data bases, analytical algorithms, and automated decision systems. These MDSs, because of their explicit presumptions and judgmental policies, give managerial decision making an uncomfortable "visibility." What was implicit, ambiguous, and mystical must become manifest if decisions are to be automated (Whisler & Shultz, 1960; 1962). Outsiders, especially system designers and programmers, must be permitted into the "inner sanctum" of managerial discretionary processes. Consequently, says Stern (1970) the development of automated decision systems is "dangerous for the manager." He claims that once the managerial decision process is specified, management will lose its aura and stature. Thus, the delegation to a computerized decision-making process may be considered by management as "threatening" (Radford, 1973).

Some authors do not agree that automated MDSs will soon be making decisions for management. Anshen (1960) believes it sheer "science fiction" to assume managerial discretionary activities will be seized by programmed "black boxes." Ignizio and Shannon (1971) doubt that automated decision systems can displace managerial judgmental ability. Boulden and Buffa (1970) do not consider MDSs a "panacea" for problem solving, but these systems may still retain a certain appeal to management, since they do not necessitate any essential changes in a manager's role: thus the manager "remains the focus of the decision-making process, with a high premium placed on his judgment and intuition." Shaul (1964) believes that with MDSs making routine decisions, managers will be liberated to devote time to conspicuous decisions involving high risk. The executive can really rely on his hunches and intuition in these rather uncertain situations, and feel omniscient and omnipotent. This is more in line with idealistic managerial decision-making strategy for top executives (Porter & Ghiselli, 1957). Jackson (1970) reports that many middle managers claim an expansion of their discretionary abilities due to the introduction of a computer-based system. Dale (1964) declares that decision-making authority will remain decentralized in spite of an increased centralization of automation. Specifically, he says, "no real change in the locus of important decisions has occurred so far as a result of computerization." Finally, Drucker (1966) argues that MDS "will not eliminate middle managers—it will force them to learn to make decisions."

CONSEQUENCES OF MANAGEMENT DECISION SYSTEMS FOR THE DECISION MAKER

Vergin (1967) claims that the current information supplied by an MIS permits management to make better informed, more itemized, and more rapid decisions. Stern (1970) seems to agree. Burck (1964a) believes that the computer will tremendously improve human cognition, and he refers to it as the "Universal Disciplinarian." One of the primary advantages he mentions is that a computer imparts to a decision maker a tendency to structure many "inherently insoluble problems." In other words, the system is likely to make the decision maker more "risky" because of diffusion of responsibility. If the outcome is not as it should be, the manager can readily blame the computerized system or its designer. Burlingame (1961) mentions that a major impact of MISs will be an improved decision-making process, and not its mechanization. This seems similar to Burck's statement that the computer is constantly improving management's capacity to make more precise decisions. Carroll (1967) claims that computerized systems have two important effects upon decision making. First, they provide rapid access to current data bases. Second, they inherently yield novel means for problem solving based on their "pseudo-cognitive powers." According to Leavitt and Whisler (1958), one of the major advantages that MISs offer management is the minimization of risky decisions in noisy intraorganizational communications. With computer-based systems, it is easier for the decision maker to choose more objectively among many alternatives by employing quantitative criteria (Jayant, 1974). Vandell (1970) suggests that MISs will minimize judgmental errors and augment sound problem solving.

Decisions that were once made judgmentally by management can now be executed automatically by the computer through simplified algorithmic routines. One salient result of this mechanization is the "depersonalization" of the discretionary process. The manager now passively receives alpha-numeric or graphic cues that elicit his judgmental response. The once omnipotent manager is now manipulated by the mechanized Machiavelli. He now has "a machine for a boss" (Whisler & Shultz, 1960). According to Argyris (1971), such programmed decision systems will probably make the manager feel like a "psychological failure." The computer will now be defining decision objectives, now specifying alternative goal paths, and now evaluating the decision maker's performance! The manager must be completely responsive to an automated system that is entirely external and foreign to his inherent intuition and instincts. In short, it seems that the manager will no longer be able to exercise any essential executive functions. To say the least, he will be a frustrated person. Decisions traditionally made by managerial "rules of thumb" will now be exercised according to programmed algorithms and heuristics (Anshen, 1969; Vergin, 1967). The manager is caught in a sort of "double bind." If he agrees to use an MDS in order to become a more objective and effective decision maker, he simultaneously "damns himself" by forsaking his intrinsic managerial functions.

It definitely appears that the manager's job, his daily experience, and his training will be affected by the introduction of MIS. But, according to Simon (1967), the attempt to specify exact role relationships between manager and computer is a bit premature. Obviously, many repetitive decisions will be made by MDSs. Consequently, "the craft of management," especially in regard to decision making, will be significantly altered. Whatever expertise management has developed to make decisions will undoubtedly be challenged by programmed systems (Whisler & Shultz, 1962). Normally self-sufficient decision makers will have to learn to adapt and to utilize the computer's capacity (Vergin & Grimes, 1964). Thus, many curricula should be altered in order to give adequate exposure to this "powerful instrument of decision" (Anshen, 1960). The computer is not eliminating managerial jobs; it is restructuring these positions so that managers are more free to dedicate their efforts to more important problems (Drucker, 1966). This new computer-based technology has the potential "for enriching and enlarging rather than diminishing the job of the manager" (Anshen, 1960). The decision maker who relies primarily on intuition, guesswork, and hunch must acquire the capacity to minimize risks by exercising computer-tested optimal strategies (Reynolds, 1969; Rowe, 1962). Managers must familiarize themselves with model building via remote terminal, through which they can explore and evaluate the results of tentative decisions before they are put into effect (Murdick, 1972).

Not everybody agrees that MIS has had an impact on management. Brady (1967) thinks that these systems have had no noticeable effect upon decision makers not only because of the intrinsic complexity of their tasks, but also because of the unquantifiable nature of much of their input. In situations where computers can make significant contributions, many managers are not making maximum use of them for several reasons:

1. Lack of appreciation (or even education) on the part of many top and middle managers regarding the ways computers and computer information can be used in making decisions.
2. A defensive attitude on the part of some top managers regarding the threat that the computer presents to their decision-making functions and to their prerogatives of exercising "managerial judgment."
3. A lag in the development of currently practicable systems which are geared primarily to assisting top managers in making decisions.

4. A hesitancy on the part of some top managers to formally identify the criteria which they wish used in decision making.
5. A tendency for top executives to wait for other firms to incur the expense and risk of pioneering and testing new areas of computer applications. (p. 76)

Kanter (1972) claims that much of management's mistrust of automated decision making has to do with the inability of these systems to capture and incorporate "executive sensitivity or gut feel," the nonquantifiable data that are important parts of managerial discretion. It is very hard to express managerial value judgments through a computer (Jones, 1970). This suggests that the role of the manager as decision maker will not necessarily be usurped by a skillfully designed automated system (Beged-Dov, 1967), especially in situations where management "loathes delegating" its decision making function (Eilon, 1969). The system shall not "encroach on their domain of responsibility."

COMPUTERIZED DECISION SYSTEMS AND INFORMATION OVERLOAD

Carlson and Gilman (1974) define information as "a resource of processed data that reduces the uncertainty in an organization, that is perceived in terms of images and patterns, and that is an essential ingredient in making a decision." Schroder, Driver, and Streufert (1967) consider information anything that changes objective or subjective probabilities or utilities, independent of whether certitude is increased or decreased. It should be stressed that the accumulation of data does not necessarily yield information. In order to have information, data must somehow be processed, interpreted, and related to purposeful objectives (Bassett, 1971). Data reduction or compression can be achieved by "aggregation and summarization." Combining or aggregating data eliminates much of the superfluous specifics sometimes involved in reams of data. Condensing or summarizing data minimizes output by producing "meaningfully processed" and interpretable data (Carlson & Gilman, 1974).

Vazsonyi (1973a) cautions against the "semantic pollution in information systems." According to Hill (1965), semantics should be considered, since these factors can undermine the effectiveness of an MIS. Ackoff (1967) asserts that the emphasis in designing MISs should be placed on purging irrelevant information. Otherwise, he claims, undue attention will probably be given to the "generation, storage, and retrieval" of irrelevant and unrefined information. Where interpretation of information is a function of other contextual information (what Slovic, Fleissner, & Bauman, [1972] call the "configurality" effect), the MIS will be manipulating and summarizing useless and meaningless material. The cost of automating such uninterpretable and unpurified information undoubtedly goes beyond the point of diminishing returns. This kind of information is definitely not worth the purchase (Fried & Peterson, 1969). To say the least, it does not present "relevant states of nature" to the decision maker so that he can minimize risk. Why should the manager seek this sort of information if the cost incurred in maintaining an MIS is much more than the probable payoff (Edwards & Slovic, 1965)? A decision maker is most unlikely to seek information from an automated system that he considers irrelevant to his needs. The manager in this situation will probably not value the information if it is improbable that an MIS will increase the likelihood of his making a better decision (Lanzetta & Kanareff, 1962). The amount of available information may be augmented because of automated systems; however, in this circumstance, the difficulty involved in attempting to decipher reams of irrelevant material may be prohibitive.

According to Daniel (1961), a problem that plagues many managers is lack of sufficient information. Much of the available information is not relevant to the tasks of specifying objectives, defining alternatives, and making decisions. Because, at times, too many goals and possibilities are revealed by an MIS, management can incur more difficulties than its cognitive ability can handle (Ackoff, 1967). Carlson and Gilman (1974) claim that "if information is not relevant, it is not information." The infinite number of facts and figures typically kept in some MISs is not true information, unless these items somehow lessen the uncertainty involved in the judgmental process. It is perfectly reasonable to assume that a well designed MIS could yield information needed for decision making more quickly and precisely than any other method now available (Baker, 1970; Rowe, 1961). Not only is a sophisticated MIS capable of providing a manager with necessary and sufficient information, but it is also capable of stimulating the decision maker to conceptualize information in novel ways (Argyris, 1971). An MIS can create a "better-informed management" in a "better-thinking management" (Koontz, 1959). Thus, managerial performance, which is related to the complexity and efficiency of information processing, would surely be improved by employing an MIS. Carlson and Gilman (1974) suggest that the complexity of information processing behavior, which is enhanced by an MIS, is a function of "(1) the amount of information used in perceptions, (2) the amount of complexity in decisions, (3) the extent of information search, and (4) the degree of innovation in behavior."

In accordance with Johnson and Derman (1970), value of information is linked to its timeliness and status of the user in the management structure. Gallagher (1974) agrees, and he indicates that "key" managerial users of MISs should be satisfied by these systems. Typically there are many shortcomings in MISs. "Reports often do not match organizational responsibilities. . . . [M]anagers do not get all the information they need for running their operations, from the formal reporting system, and at the same time it gives them information they don't need. . . . Critical factors are often buried in a mass of detail" ("A new look," 1965). If a situation of this sort exists, then a fundamental concept of information utilization proposed by Finn and Miller (1971) cannot be satisfied. They argue that the manner in which an MIS is employed must contribute to the solutions of managerial problems. An MIS can accomplish this if it is configured to the prevailing decision environment to which it inputs information. Finn and Miller describe ten fundamental principles that clarify the relationship between an information system and the decision environment:

1. Information must be acceptable to the user in order to be used. . . .
2. Information is unbiased only to the first person who receives it and not necessarily to the ultimate decision maker. . . .
3. Any information system which is to remain in existence must provide the user with something that he finds valuable in the achievement of his individual goals. . . .
4. A management system must support the actual (not stated) policies of the organization. . . .
5. Any information that is provided by an MIS will be used only if it supports the goals of the organization. . . .
6. The amount of utilization of an MIS is in direct proportion to the number of decision points in an organization. . . .
7. The amount of information utilized by an organization is in direct proportion to its risk tolerance (ability to withstand failure). . . .
8. If an information system is to remain important to an individual, it must provide him with feedback on his interaction with his environment. . . .

9. Information is not either intrinsically good or bad, valid or invalid. Any such interpretation depends on the user and its acceptability . . . to the user. . . .
10. Information is transmitted in direct proportion to its ability to be received. (pp. 18-20)

Because of "executive loneliness" caused by isolation from the very information they require, managers normally have MISs developed. Burlingame (1961) concludes that because MISs produce needed information, they can be valuable tools for minimizing managerial isolation.

Hirsch (1968) states a truism: "all decisions are made with imperfect information." He claims that several factors usually account for this: (1) the unavailability of required information, (2) the impossibility of justifying the exorbitant effort needed to obtain the necessary information, (3) the lack of knowledge concerning the whereabouts of information, and (4) the absence of information when it is urgently required. Dickson (1968) indicates that management information is intrinsically linked to judgmental processes. The primary purpose of an MIS is to provide, quickly and precisely, the information needed for decision making (Birks, 1971). Tetz (1973) thinks that at least one salient reason for installing an MIS is to surmount the limited information upon which most decisions are based. To accomplish this, it is necessary to insure that the desired information can be easily and efficiently elicited from the system upon demand (Bassett, 1971). This requires not only a properly designed MIS, but also an ability by the manager to utilize various types of computerized information systems (Bennis, 1968). The quantity and retrievability of information stored in a system is related to the state-of-the-art of computer technology and the economic costs incurred in maintaining such a system (Whisler & Shultz, 1962). Regarding cost, "the justification yardstick" for developing and maintaining these automated systems for management is measured in terms of the relationship between expense and reduction of risk (economic or otherwise) related to non- or mis-information. McDonough (1963) indicates that "some 50 percent of the costs of running our economy are information costs." Evans and Hague (1962) state that "in U.S. industry today, the gathering, storing, manipulating, and organizing of information for managing enterprises cost as much or more than does direct factory labor."

Dearden (1964) notes that many members of the management cadre are making decisions, employing "less than one-tenth of the information" that would be accessible to them without a computerized system. However, he emphasizes that inadequate information systems will not solve this problem, which is caused by lack of information. Dearden (1965) argues that computers and their associated systems are simply not being used in the most efficient way to supply management with optimal information for decision making. Different data bases are not being integrated or federated. Greiner, Leitch, and Barnes (1970) doubt that managers would significantly improve their decision-making performance, even if they were given more objective and quantified information. As management increases its use of more sophisticated decision-making technology, such as automated MISs, the likelihood increases that more information will be filtered or screened by system designers and management staffs. Because of this "filtering mechanism," management may become annoyed enough to exercise effective power to obtain the information they require.

Simon (1967) identifies "an 'information explosion' which, if less worrisome than the others [population and nuclear] still threatens to bury us under piles of paper and drown us in oceans of sounds." Carlson and Gilman (1974) point out that "information load" refers not only to content variables (timeliness, quantity, and accuracy), but also to structural variables (rate, diversity, complexity, change, organization, and presentation). Kanter (1972) claims that this information load is driven to the point of "overload" or "glut" by the capacity of computers to accumulate and generate reams of information. The amount of this information is truly a "dimensionless quantity" (Miller, 1956). It seems that everybody is using the computer to produce "tons of paper" (Drucker, 1967) or "a sea of paper" (Morton & McCosh, 1968). So much information is printed daily by these automated systems that many managers do not have sufficient time to read it. The manager's "channel capacities" (Miller, 1956) seem easily to be exceeded by system-generated information. He is usually so inundated by computer-generated information that his ability to process this input is severely taxed (Hoos, 1971).

Ackoff (1967) claims that most MISs are designed and developed on the assumption that most managers operate with a "lack of relevant information." However, he says, managers are also subjected to a superabundance of irrelevant information. Similarly, Schoderbek (1971) states that management is normally overwhelmed by "floods of irrelevant, useless, and perhaps irreliable reports." Consequently, filtration and condensation, which minimize information overload and managerial search time, are among the most important operations of an MIS. If this irrelevant information is not eliminated, then further information yielded by the MIS cannot be utilized effectively (Ackoff, 1967). At times, important information becomes intermingled with unimportant information, because MIS output is so voluminous (Stern, 1972a).

It seems that almost nothing is known about the relationship between managerial information processing and decision making. Dickson (1968) declares that "no one knows what the content of the information system should be, the form in which information should be presented to the decision maker, the media through which information should be presented, or what time availability of information should be." Individuals sometimes seek too much information, and this further complicates the creation of efficient MISs (Rapoport, 1964). Taylor (1975) finds that even older decision makers are more likely to suffer from the disfunctional effects of information overload. In order to plan MISs properly in light of the current information explosion, novel attitudes are essential, especially for the tasks of accumulating, storing, and retrieving information. These attitudes must consider "each individual component of memory—whether a human head, a correspondence file or a computer core—as a part of a total system" (Simon, 1967). If a manager fails in this, the "sixty-second man may find himself part of a 'pico-second world.'" According to Slater (1967), a manager who is not willing to master MIS techniques may suffer from "information indigestion and a blighted ego."

Koontz (1959) claims that many managers become very annoyed at the thought of further information overload due to MISs. It seems that system output is neither formatted properly, nor timed to arrive at the right moment. Also, benefits derived from the use of MISs are contingent upon the proper input to the computerized system. When unpurged data are entered into the system, a "GIGO" situation is said to exist, that is, "Garbage In—Garbage Out" (Berkowitz & Munro, 1969; Poindexter, 1969). This "input problem" is on a par with the "output problem"—information glut. A GIGO condition can cause disastrous decisions. It is likely that if incorrect input is placed within the MIS, mistaken judgments will be made. This is compounded by the fact that the presumption that management is cognizant of the nature, accuracy, and timeliness of the input it requires for decision making is seldom satisfied. On a day-to-day basis, most managers do not adequately know the extent of the discretionary activities they have to exercise. Consequently, many of them play "it 'safe' and, with respect to information [want] 'everything'" (Ackoff, 1967). This usually initiates and aggravates the GIGO condition and information overload. Many MISs are thus likely to become extremely ineffective due to a queuing effect, which is a function of "the rate of arrival of information and the time taken to process decisions" (Malcolm & Rowe, 1961; Rowe, 1962). This "delayed action list" is typically considered the maximum limit beyond which most managers cannot process complex input (Driver & Streufert, 1969). In order to develop a more effective MIS, techniques should be established to somehow predict managerial information processing abilities and requirements, so that GIGO and information overload can be minimized, if not eliminated.

4
ESSENCE OF CYBERNATED SYSTEMS

NATURE OF MAN-COMPUTER INTERACTION

"One level of the field of management information-decision systems is seldom identified, and yet is the area which is most exciting and where recent technical developments have occurred that will have far reaching consequences. This area concentrates on the development of cybernated (man-machine) interactive information-decision systems in which the manager and the information system are coupled together into a problem solving network" (Dickson, 1968). This interaction of man and computer is very pronounced in current time-sharing installations and, according to Greenless (1971), will continue to grow in importance.

Greenless (1971) and Simon (1967) observe that there is an increasing trend on the part of executives to interact with automated information storage and retrieval systems. Such systems are not limited to inert data banks: they may be dynamic and flexible, capable of conducting searches and processing information to arrive at problem solutions (Simon, 1967). Characteristics of these computerized MIS terminals that encourage managers to interact with them are their "simplicity, secrecy, conversational [ease], fast response, management control, accessibility, data availability, . . . and economy" (Boulden & Buffa, 1970). Also stimulating man-computer interaction is the trend of systems languages to more closely approximate normal conversational language (Simon, 1967). The "real-time" aspect of the man-computer interface allows decision makers greater ease in planning, as well as the ability to evaluate more alternate plans (Carroll, 1966; Jones, 1970). Adaptability and flexibility in problem identification and definition, as well as access to both large amounts of data and vast computational power, are additional attributes of cybernated systems that enhance the utility of MIS console usage for managers (Morton & McCosh, 1968). While interactive terminals appear to be most useful in solving structured problems, Morton (1971) mentions that they may also be economically feasible tools for executives to use for certain groups of unstructured problems, especially "where the problems are hard to define explicitly and where solutions involve complex strategies."

Although the potential for man-computer interactive systems is great, much research will be needed before it is reached. Diebold (1965) declares that much progress in enhancing the man-machine interface will occur, and that the main impediment will not be lack of technical knowledge, but rather a lack of management knowledge, planning, and effort. Similarly, Pryor (1969) describes the state-of-the-art in time sharing as "a conglomerate of third-generation hardware, second-generation software, first-generation terminals, and 'zero' generation management enlightenment." Schewe (1973) expresses an equivalent view when he says that the "MIS/system user interface is highly interdependent and only as strong as its weakest link." He goes on to suggest that a "management information system . . . is really only as good as the system user. The information system is merely a machine full of potential information whose value is realized as the system user puts the system to use." This is contrary to how man-machine information systems have been developed. Emphasis has usually been placed on the hardware, with little attention given to the needs of the user (Baker, 1970). It should "be seen that machines are not supplanting human thinking and judgment. They are merely adjuncts to persons, and thinking and creativity are still means to an end rather than an end within themselves" (Megginson, 1963).

The interactive aspect of the man-machine system tends to impose upon or control the jobs of the users. Kaufman (1965) stresses that the "major function of man within automated systems is: (a) to monitor the operation in order to receive information relevant to the system operation; and (b) to carry out the necessary feedback control operations on the basis of information received." Yntema and Torgerson (1961) cite two solutions to the dilemma of how best to combine the system's speed and man's flexible judgment, without unduly sacrificing too much of either. "One typical solution is to have the machine assemble and present to the man the facts he will probably want in reaching a decision. . . . Another is to let the machine make the decision according to the comparatively simple rules that can be programmed into it, but require man to monitor the situation and countermand the machine's orders if he finds them too foolish." Any such constraints imposed on the user by the system designers may be critical determinants of user performance. More and more managers who have access to information systems will be expected to make use of these systems in performance of their duties. However, acceptability and availability of MISs do not automatically result in the effective use of these systems. System characteristics—real-time, time-sharing, natural and extendable languages, and graphic display devices—appear to have a favorable influence on user performance with the system. Other developments such as the interconnecting or networking of systems, which will require new methods of documentation, user communication, and more extensive training, may hinder human performance (Mayer, 1970).

The primary purpose of tactical information systems is to provide decision makers or commanders with intelligence upon which to base their decisions. In military decision situations, it is not uncommon for choices to be arrived at through a group or team effort. "Thus it is important for system designers to know the extent to which decision-making behavior within a military information system may be modified by characteristics of individuals and by social influences of a group. The group factor complicates the problem of specifying optimum criteria for decision-making in an information system context" (Mayer, 1970). Mayer also suggests that constraints imposed by the system on man-machine communication, as well as man-man communication, will affect the decision-making ability of humans interacting with the system. Other factors influencing human interaction with MIS include task taxonomy (whether open ended or fixed) and human problem-solving style. Sackman (1970), for example, reports that in real-time interaction between the system and the user "better performers tend to use more computer time for open-ended tasks whereas better performance of fixed problems showed the reverse trend."

Certain deterrents to effective human performance may occur with the widespread use of interacting terminals for problem solving. Specifically, the tendency to present only one side or aspect of an issue may increase. This failure to expose users to contrasting views of a problem may limit their ability to think and logically consider alternatives (Mitroff, 1975). Also, the tendency of decision makers to think concretely—to use knowledge that is actually displayed by the terminal and to employ it in the format in which it is presented—may be a hindrance to the most effective performance of the human component in interfacing with the system. Slovic (1972) emphasizes this point when he states that knowledge that "has to be stored in memory, inferred from the explicit display, or transformed tends to be discounted or ignored." Because MDSs are often composed of only a simplification of the total number of relationships and assumptions concerning a problem, Jones (1970) stresses that it may be wise to allow these systems to be used only by the decision makers closest to the problem being considered, since they will be most aware of alternatives not adequately dealt with by the decision system. This suggests that MDSs may be most effectively used at the lower managerial levels. If so, the use of rapid conversational interaction between man and computer may best be suited to dealing with routine problem solving, instead of creative and novel problem solving at the terminal (Sackman, 1970).

MANAGER-COMPUTER INTERFACE

The interactive relationship between man and the computer depends on certain critical factors, one of which is the peripheral equipment of the computer. The development of new types of less costly terminals and other hardware is increasing the flexibility of MDSs. Other than peripheral equipment and the human element, the only major limitation to on-line, real-time decision systems is the operating software (Boulden & Buffa, 1970). Of these factors, terminal-type hardware appears to be the strong link in the chain making up computerized decision systems. As improvements are made in software and breakthroughs (such as microwave, microfilm, and optical scanning) occur in communications, further advancement toward the realization of management information and decision systems will occur (Dickson, 1968). Also, developments such as cost reductions and better random-access files and memories are making integrated data bases more feasible (Diebold, 1965).

Managerial problem solving, which is supposed to occur at the interface with the computer system, has been described as the search for possible alternatives until one or more potentially attractive solution is found. Then the decision maker enters an exploratory phase, manipulating variables and analyzing the resultant conditions. "The computer routines should present displays to help the manager find an attractive approximate answer; see the strengths, weaknesses, and opportunities of a particular answer; and make the series of small modifications that turn a merely acceptable solution into a good solution" (Jones, 1970). The terminal currently most conducive to the achievement of this process appears to be the graphic display console. These CRT (cathode ray tube) devices offer the advantages of quietness, adaptability, and quickness, which make them very desirable for use by managers wishing to examine situations in new ways (Jones, 1970). Morton and McCosh (1968) stress the fact that users understand graphic presentations far better than numeric output. Also, Miller (1969) emphasizes that graphic display devices are one of the most powerful new developments in machine capabilities that make decision analysis more efficient.

These CRTs can provide a user direct interaction with the computer via a light pen. Thus it is easy for a decision maker to direct the computer to quickly calculate new values of variables that satisfy the conditions and/or revisions of the graphic information displayed. The exploratory decision-making capabilities of this type of system are much greater than those in systems that employ static graphic displays. This type of flexible, computer-controlled graphic console does not replace managerial judgment, "but rather, enhances it by providing immediate quantitative answers to the executive's intuitive questions about the operation of his business" (Miller, 1969). Morton (1971) also emphasizes that the display terminal has no value except as a tool to aid the decision process by providing improved communication, by making available computerized power, and by permitting access to structured data. Organizations are moving to utilize the advantages of this type of system, as shown by Litton Industries' plan to install CRT picture phone screens in executive offices, so that decision makers can query the computer directly (Kegerreis, 1971). "In summary, the interactive computer graphics devices and accompanying software comprise a judgment aid with the following properties: 1) The judgement process, which is covert, internal and subjective, is clarified and externalized so that it can be examined and understood. 2) Desired changes in judgement policy, motivated by discussion, change of values, or by the feedback about judgement policy from the graphics device can be specified and executed with perfect consistency" (Stewart, West, Hammond, & Kreith, 1975). But a major impediment to the widespread use of these devices is their high cost. As with most new technology, though, costs are expected to decline dramatically, and the devices will likely become more economical in the near future (Jones, 1970; Joseph, 1971). Also, care must be taken to insure that these devices are designed to facilitate the input-output styles not only of individuals, but also of small groups. Because decisions are often made by small groups, the social aspects of decision making must not be overlooked. The CRT console should display figures and graphics large enough for simultaneous viewing by decision teams of at least six to eight persons (Jones, 1970).

Although graphic display consoles are a means of optimizing man-computer interaction and communications, much work has also been done, and is continuing, in the utilization of more natural or conversational languages. If these on-going research endeavors produce feasible results, then direct voice input, rather than teletype or light pen input, would likely be developed. This would further simplify the task of decision makers in communicating directly with the computer (Mayer, 1970).

The importance of user reaction to an information system is one of the critical aspects to be considered in the design of any MIS.

Knowledge of how users will react to systems is often extremely limited, and consequently, assumptions are usually made regarding users' behavior. These assumptions, even ones that depict the users as reacting rationally, are often ridiculous (Vazsonyi, 1974). "In designing complex systems, regardless of our good intentions, we can often create a situation which becomes intolerable for the human being and as a result he either leaves the system or, if he cannot, he subordinates himself to the system and ceases to play the role which is the ultimate role of men in man-machine systems, to see to it that the system works" (Jordan, 1962).

Mayer (1970) also believes that one of the greatest challenges facing designers of information systems is to make certain that the system's attributes are acceptable to users. Often the user reacts to the instantaneous response the system supplies to his question by immediately posing another question that is again answered almost instantaneously. This user reaction, to keep the computer busy, is not only a waste of computer time, but also of user time (Goldston, 1970). Rapoport (1964) suggests that a decision maker's behavior may be influenced by the tendency to trust and follow the computer's decisions, and by the feeling that the computer is less likely to err or cheat him than a human. Problems are caused not only by the new technology comprising the computerized information system, but also by the way the system is introduced to the people who must use it. Inadequate justification of the purpose and usefulness of the MIS and insufficient training and familiarization in using it often engender in users feelings of resentment and actual resistance to implementation of the system. Of all the factors influencing the quality of man-machine interaction, the one dealt with the most in the literature is that of time spans.

ESSENTIALS OF TIME SPANS

The initial usage of computers involved batch processing of data. These types of computers and their systems offered users only initial set-up costs and slow turn-around time for results. Due to these factors, batch-type systems did not lend themselves to managerial use for dynamic, unstructured problem solving. Rather, decision makers often continued to rely on older manual information systems and intuition (Morton, 1971). The extended time factor involved in batch processing was often unavoidable, and little benefit could be accrued for shortening it. Several trends, however, spurred the elimination of the intrinsic need for such delays. Increased emphasis on planning that requires time, together with the inclination of organizations to grow larger and become more centralized, has stimulated a change in the function of data processing systems from inert recorders of history to dynamic controllers of current operations (Martin, 1965; Rader, 1968). This has become possible by designing interacting computers that process data in real-time, thus permitting managers to probe unstructured problem areas by asking a wide range of specific questions, testing out plans, and quickly supplying information to both subordinates and superiors (Morton, 1971). Also contributing to the spread of real-time systems is improved computer technology, especially in computer-communications systems (Murdick, 1972).

Various descriptions of real-time systems have been presented in the literature. The following statements regarding these systems are typical: "they will reflect important and routine events as they occur" (Diebold, 1965); "data will be maintained 'on-line', . . . data will be updated as events occur, . . . the computer can be interrogated from remote terminals . . . connected to a large-scale computer with a data bank containing all of the relevant information in the company" (Dearden, 1966); "the computer . . . responds to inquiries and processing requests in so short a time frame that decisions controlling current operations can be made from these responses" (Murdick, 1972); "at any one time we are able to query the computer and receive up-to-date information on any desired phase of the business" (Pattillo, 1969); and "the system responds while you wait, so to speak" (Carroll, 1966). It seems clear, then, that the most salient advantage of real-time systems is their speed in processing information. This speed gives users access to up-to-date and instant information from which immediate decisions can be made.

The most common form of fast response system is that of time sharing, which has several noticeable advantages. Because the user is on-line at the terminal, the problem being considered may be broken down easily into understandable and manageable parts. Also, due to a time-sharing terminal's easy access to the central computer and the system's very short turn-around time, relatively efficient noninterrupted and massed problem solving and learning by the user is possible. Immediate feedback of results at the terminal is much more desirable than the turn-around time associated with batch processing of data, which imposes a forced interruption on the user that can increase his forgetting and often requires additional reacquaintance and warm-up time (Sackman, 1970). Another advantage of real-time systems, especially time-sharing ones, is that the terminal can be made more accessible to executives whose decision processes cannot be rigidly scheduled. Having a remote console situated in his office is ideal for a decision maker who must seek information at irregular or unpredictable times (Jones, 1970). Though the concept of real-time is closely associated with time-sharing or on-line types of systems, it is not exclusive to these applications. The extent to which information is real-time depends on the rate at which information requirements change. If data can be reported and conveniently used every month, for example, then a batch process information system may in effect be real-time, at least inasmuch as the output is available when needed.

Although the alleged advantages and potential payoffs of real-time information systems are legion, several authors recognize problems and practical limitations to this type of systems utility. Dearden (1966), for example, believes that the supposed benefits of real-time information systems for management are founded on three false assumptions. First, a real-time MIS will not necessarily give a manager any degree of improved control in the operations of the organization. As a result, it will not aid in reducing the insecurity that a manager feels because he does not know everything there is to know about the organization. What is needed to improve management control is an information system in conjunction with improved selection and training of personnel. Second, the aura of scientific management that envelops the executive who has a computer terminal in his office may be somewhat illusory. The manager's time is probably more effectively spent in managing and letting others play "Liberace at the console." Third, management control systems are not higher-level representations of logistics systems. Hence, the advantage that real-time methods have in logistics systems—increased speed in processing and transmitting vast quantities of data—cannot be projected onto management control systems, since data handling is not a critical problem in this type of system.

Another limitation of fast response, real-time MISs is the design objective to obtain the fastest possible response time. This designed-in minimum-response time will often vary, because it depends on such factors as total load upon the system and the computational time needed for the particular task at hand. Simon (1966) suggests that instead of letting the system's response time vary according to the conditions at hand, its output should come either immediately before or after a fixed time. It would be more efficient if delays were made long enough so that the user could redirect his attention to secondary tasks, instead of sitting idly at the terminal. Simon argues that a user cannot efficiently move from one simple task to another, unless at least several minutes are allotted for the alternate activity. For other complex problems, a user probably needs at least an hour effectively to redirect his activity away from the terminal. Yntema and Torgerson (1961) are also concerned with the fast response time of on-line systems. If the system should output a sudden succession of items or decisions, the user may become a bottleneck or be so overloaded that his performance deteriorates.

Another writer who discusses the desirability and suitability of the fast response systems is Sackman (1970). He observes: "There is increasing evidence that rapid-fire, conversationally paced interaction between the user and the computer is fine for routine problem steps, for verification of preconceived and well-understood ideas, and for minor or tactical problem-solving; but strategic problem-solving, major insights into a problem which leads to major innovation, like good wine requires longer periods for maturation." He also feels that the term "man-computer symbiosis" may be a misleading description of man-computer problem-solving activity. As an alternative interpretation, Sackman suggests that the computer and its associated information capabilities be considered a tactical tool, assisting humans in problem-solving activities where the user supplies the direction and strategic intelligence.

Another variable possibly influencing the performance of users of real-time systems is the way they are billed or charged for their interaction with and usage of the system. Clearly, a user's strategy could differ drastically depending on whether he were charged solely on the basis of how much central processor time he used, or on the basis of his on-line time. If billed for only central processing time, the user may tend to work at the terminal with only an approximate idea of the problem in mind. He may then proceed at an easy pace, having freedom to work with paper and pencil. Conversely, if the user is charged according to his time at the terminal, he may have greater incentive to plan, write, and de-bug his programs and other work before reaching the console. Also, a user in this situation will be less likely to allow interruptions of his on-line work. As most organizations use measures of both on-line and central processing time to determine computing costs, the issue boils down to the unresolved question of how the user's behavior in interacting with the system depends on the weighting of different time measures (Nickerson, Elkind, & Carbonell, 1968).

FUTURE OF MANAGER-COMPUTER SYMBIOSIS

Many authors have donned the robes of soothsayer, and have forecast the future of man-computer interaction. Jayant (1974), for example, predicts that "it will be possible to provide line managers the most up-to-date information through terminals installed in their own offices. They are bound to demand the development of systems to fulfill this which so far has not been possible to satisfy. . . .

[Also,] since the users themselves can get their results by querying the computer, the line managers will feel themselves closer to the computer and are likely to be more willing to accept the results they receive on their terminals as a result of their query."

Currently, the state of the art has made more feasible geographically decentralized time-sharing computer systems, including civilian airline reservation and elaborate military command and control display systems (Baran, 1965). Improved technology in communications, terminals, and switching systems will render future information systems "more nearly parallel to the real flow of information within the organization" (Diebold, 1969a). Consequently, direct conversational communication between man and computer will become possible for nearly all management levels, thus eliminating the need for printed reports. In an earlier article, Diebold (1965) predicts that voice and data communications will be revolutionized in organizations, nations, and the world by advances in technology such as video-phones, and by developments in integrating computer systems. Miller (1965) conjectures that just "as we can plug our electrical appliances into the wall and draw power from a central station, so in the future we shall be able to plug our typewriters into the telephone system and draw intelligence from a central computer." Future developments in technology will give us electronic devices that "enable people to interact directly and personally and to perceive the world more immediately and totally than before when they had to work through the intermediary of print. As a result, center-margin (superior-subordinate, empire-colony) relationships have been becoming increasingly diffuse" (Reynolds, 1969).

With the development of time-sharing capabilities, organizations may incorporate parallel levels of information, so that subordinates may have access to the same information that supervisors have. Unless the terminals are controlled or restricted, there is nothing to prevent the executive from being second-guessed on every decision. Subordinate access to information, instead of generating personnel problems, could be used beneficially. There would no longer be any technological reasons why all employees could not participate in the decision-making process (Blose & Goetze, 1971). Blose and Goetze also suggested that very "often people within an organization need direction because they lack a macro-view. Information available on-line will aid people to manage themselves." Not all will take advantage of this asset of the system, but those who do will be able to advance, and not stagnate in their current jobs. Before these speculations and lofty goals can be met, however, much study and research needs to be done.

Many authors have cited this lack of research and stressed the need for detailed study of the problems associated with man-computer interaction in decision-making systems. Of the possible societal consequences of man-computer interaction, or "cybernation" as he calls it, Dickson (1968) warns that research is needed to determine what problems will be caused by the increased educational needs of a computer-based society. Also, he cautions that the possible formation of an "information elite" should be studied. Sackman (1970) contends that narrow "technical considerations and immediate cost constraints dominated computer technology . . . [in the past] and still dominate it today, in large part at the expense of human ease, convenience, and social effectiveness. . . . As things stand now, the user is the forgotten man, and the general public stands to suffer in the long run from this pervasive experimental and humanistic lag in information services." He further suggests that the use of paper-and-pencil tests, though relatively low in validity, could be a good cost-effective means of studying user skills and individual differences in performance in man-computer communications.

Morton (1971) also points out that there has been little experience with, and even less research done, in the field of interactive computing. Hard data on both the capabilities of the computer and the function of man in the system are essential if progress toward resolving both the hardware difficulties and the human problems is to be made. Suggesting that future research is essential, Morton (1971) points to the following critical areas needing attention:

1. Software requirements for interactive terminals.
2. Nature of the interface between manager and device.
3. Central computer requirements to support terminals.
4. Problem characteristics to which the system can be applied.
5. Type of user able to work with the system. (p. 10)

Up to now the majority of "the contributions made by social scientists to the understanding of the effects of technical change [due to man-machine cybernation], particularly the effects on the management process, [have been] . . . descriptive and general" (Walker, 1968).

Baker (1970) refers to five crucial functional areas needing experimental attention if anticipated man-computer problems in military information systems are to be successfully resolved: these systems will have to (1) evaluate incoming data as to its relevance, believability, importance, and eventual usage; (2) convert the incoming data for input into computer memory; (3) input the transformed data into computer storage for later analysis and output; (4) evaluate the displayed output; (5) choose courses of action founded on the information outputed by the system and from other sources. Research on how these factors influence human performance is especially necessary in the military environment, where personnel are constantly being turned over or transferred. This, taken with the fact that strategic and tactical decisions are frequently made by groups of men, tends to aggravate the difficulty of human factors, which is often less pronounced in less complicated or less dynamic systems (Mayer, 1970).

It has been suggested in the literature (Ansoff, 1965) that eventually most nonprogrammable decisions may come within the capabilities of computer-based decision systems, and that the choice whether or not to displace decision makers will be based primarily on economic considerations. The most important decision, however, may not be that between man or computer, but will have to do, instead, with construction of man-computer systems that draw on the unique abilities of each: the human's talent for setting goals, constructing hypotheses, and selecting criteria; and the computer's ability to examine alternatives rapidly. As Morton and McCosh (1968) say, the objective "is to combine the manipulative power of the electronic computer, the simplicity and convenience of the computer terminal, and the business skill of the manager to arm him with the most up-to-date, accurate, and appropriate cost information that can be obtained with modern technology." According to Peace and Easterby (1973), the two fundamental reasons why this objective has yet to be reached are that man is being dealt with as if he were just another hardware component of the system, and that there is in general "a lack of perception of the nature of the man-computer relationship." They further stress that methods are needed to help systematically develop the criteria or specifications for specific man-computer interacting systems. Accomplishing this may be difficult, however, because management has often been instructed in meticulously examining the validity of its data, but is often unable to evaluate the validity of its information. This is because information is data that has been evaluated with respect to human goals: of this there is limited cognizance and understanding (Finn & Miller, 1971).

2

IMPLICATIONS OF COMPUTER-BASED MANAGEMENT INFORMATION SYSTEMS FOR ORGANIZATIONAL STRUCTURE AND PROCESSES

5
IMPLICATIONS OF COMPUTER-BASED MANAGEMENT INFORMATION SYSTEMS FOR ORGANIZATIONAL STRUCTURE

COMPUTERIZED INFORMATION SYSTEMS AND ORGANIZATIONAL STRUCTURE

As our society becomes larger and more technological, increased dependence on the vast data handling capabilities of modern high speed electronic computers is occurring. The demands of the competitive environment and the volume of data handling experienced by almost all organizations in our society have stimulated the development and utilization of MISs. These systems are being used to assist decision makers in performing their tasks with greater accuracy and speed. For the most part, however, these MISs have been designed, developed, and implemented by firms with little understanding of the consequences for organizational structures and processes.

It is not that effects were unanticipated or unexpected, for many writers recognized that the introduction of an MIS into an enterprise would generate substantial and sometimes radical change within that organizational framework (Leavitt & Whisler, 1958; Lee, 1967; Moan, 1973; Vergin, 1967). As Whisler and Shultz (1962) point out, "although the impress of the computer will vary from firm to firm . . . the first wave of this impact will be on: (1) the existing organization structure in each firm, (2) the current bundle of jobs at the managerial level, in terms of both number of jobs and job context, and (3) the present structure of authority in the management hierarchy." Although such consequences are expected, there is still little agreement or consensus regarding the exact effects of MISs on the structure of organizations and the style of management.

Ignizio and Shannon (1971) review the literature that attempts to forecast the influence of MIS on organizational structure and management. They group the varied and divergent prognostications into several categories. The first reveals that organizations will likely develop into an hourglass structure with fewer levels of management overall, fewer middle managers, more top managers, and a greater ratio of skilled workers to unskilled workers. The other group of projections forecasts a bulging pyramidal structure in which there are more levels of management and a greater increase in the ratio of skilled workers to unskilled workers. Besides these two divergent views, there are also those according to which the time-honored pyramidal structure will not change significantly, except for an increase in the ratio of skilled to unskilled labor. The consensus, then, is that there will be an increase in the ratio of skilled to unskilled employees.

Simon (1960a), Leavitt and Whisler (1958), and Ignizio and Shannon (1971) note that most of the predictions of the hourglass structure are based upon the following assumptions: accelerating use of the computer will require a restructuring of activities in different divisions and levels of the organization; MISs can be used to perform a greater number of routine decisions that management has made in the past; and, finally, more responsibility for the creative functions of planning and innovating will shift to upper management. This should centralize control of the decision process.

Anshen (1960) and Rader (1968) forecast bulging pyramidal organizational structures in response to MIS use. They believe that, similar to past trends, an increase in size and complexity of organizations will continue to cause an increase in the size of managerial staffs, as well as stimulate the formation of new levels of management. Also, they predict that computer applications such as MISs will only be useful for routine, repetitive, and programmable decisions. Thus, such managerial tasks as setting goals, making complex or novel decisions, and implementing and evaluating these decisions are areas that will be relatively unaffected by MIS (Ignizio & Shannon, 1971).

Ignizio and Shannon conclude that the following organizational changes will occur due to MIS implementation: "an increased growth of staff as opposed to line positions . . . the use of more sophisticated management techniques and quantitative analyses methods, [and] more intellectual activity throughout the organization, versus manual or clerical [activity]." Also, they predict the expansion of "sophisticated management control systems . . . [and] an increasing use of the matrix management concept in the middle management levels." These trends imply an organizational structure similar to the hourglass model.

Predicting the failure of old organizational methods and procedures to remain competitive, Haberstroh (1961) suggests that increased experimentation with organizational forms will occur. Also, he stresses that novel methods of information processing will be a salient factor in determining which new organizational forms will be most appropriate and cost-effective. Likewise, Whisler (1970a) foresees continued changes in organizational structure and functional alignment. However, he believes that the question of whether or not organizations will become more centralized in response to MIS usage will not be answered for some time. He forecasts a continued blurring of the strict distinction between line and staff workers, and a further reduction in the number of clerical workers. And he identifies as an important, but as yet unresolved, issue the appropriate role and location of an MIS within the organization.

Contary to many of the previously cited assumptions—that computers and MISs could cause some form of change within organizations—it has been suggested that computerized information systems will not be a major determinant for inducing changes in organizational structure (Kanter, 1972). Rather, an MIS may only function as a catalyst for organizational change, not as its true cause. That is, the computer will be used by an organization as a means of proceeding along whatever tack, either centralization or decentralization, the organization has decided on. Stieber (1957) expresses a similar view when he comments that "it is not possible to generalize about the effects of . . . [MIS] on the centralization or decentralization of business operations. It is to be expected that, as computers of varying capabilities and prices become available, companies will have considerable freedom in selecting the type that will best serve their needs and operational policies." Still, most authors agree that MIS will be a major force shaping organizations in the future. Yet, despite the many and varied predictions regarding the effects of MISs upon organizations, there is little objective and reliable data concerning the influence on organizational form (Lucas, 1973).

Despite a wide variety of opinions, there seems to be a consensus that technology, especially MISs, will necessitate a rearrangement of organizational structures into shapes that are not as yet obvious (Whisler, 1965). As early as 1959, Jasinski stresses that changes in technology generally affect organizational relationships. He warns that the imposition of a technology, which accents certain diagonal and horizontal structures upon an organization, may cause difficulties. This may be particularly true where the organizational structure emphasizes vertical relationships. He recognizes that new technologies have caused reorganization of certain departments, in order to harmonize them with the specific technology. Usually, however, such revisions are restricted to a subunit of the organization, or to parts of the organization where most pressure is being exerted. This may directly affect the impact of the MIS.

Up to now, the majority of computer applications in organizations have served as replacements for low-order, highly routine human functions (accounting and data processing) or as aids for not too complex, mid-level decision problems. Few organizational applications have taken advantage of the computer's "more elaborate, many level, real time systems-type programs, or nonhierarchical (at the top) humanoid heuristic programs, both of which appear appropriate for certain classes of more complex, ill-defined tasks" (Klahr & Leavitt, 1967). Instead of limiting applications of MISs, more stress should be placed on redesigning entire organizational structures to match the advanced forms of technology, such as MISs that are being developed for use in both factory and office work (Cooper & Foster, 1971).

Further attempts to adapt organizations to an MIS may have particular organizational implications. Boettinger (1969) hypothesizes that the nature of future organizations will be very different from, and much more innovative than, current managerial organizations. Furthermore, he suggests that, in the future, procedures developed for designing technology may be applied to the design of organizations. These techniques will consider the technological aspect of management, which usually has been ignored. That is, technology may be evaluated as central to organizational and managerial processes, instead of as something to be circumvented or resisted in order to maintain the status quo. Boettinger also forecasts changes "in supervisory arrangements and work assignments, designed to develop individual motivation to adapt" as a necessary step in accommodating an organization to a specific technological environment. Any future restructuring of an organization in response to an MIS, however, will be contingent on the ability of top management to rearrange the traditionally compartmentalized structure of organizations. Reorganizing in response to MIS usage may be especially important in organizations dealing with highly educated or creative personnel. In such situations, the tenets of authority, command, and responsibility might not be the best principles of organization. Instead, an MIS might accentuate the need for an organization based on the principles of knowledge, judgment, and expectations (Drucker, 1956).

It is not exactly clear what organizational forms will emerge in the future as a result of MIS. Haberstroh (1961) predicts that the structures that first evolve may "be largely a matter of historical accident, although conscious experimentation cannot be entirely ruled out." Simon (1960b, 1960c) thinks that organizations of the future will be structured in three layers. The substratum will consist of the systems of production and distribution. Upon this foundation will be a layer of automated and programmed decision processes, which regulate the lower physical systems. At the pinnacle of the organization will be heuristic and nonprogrammed decision methods, which govern and readjust the lower level processes.

Possibly, the impact of MISs on organizations will be great enough to render the usual methods of dealing with change ineffective. In the past, it was not uncommon for managers to reconcile the differences between organizational structure and technology by modifying the technology to match the organizational structure. Alternately, managers could attempt to maintain both technology and structure by introducing mechanisms (paperwork, transfers, social activities, and so on) to minimize the mismatch between structure and technology (Jasinski, 1959). In the near future, however, the technological impact of MISs may necessitate the change of organizational structure in order to make explicit and to reinforce the relationships needed by the technology for maximum efficiency.

If the implementation of MISs is to cause substantial change in organizations, what binding force will be used to restructure these organizations? Diebold (1969b) believes that the information system itself will become the heart of the organizational structure. Information processing, he stresses, will become a major activity in all levels of management, from production to planning. Similarly, Whisler (1970b) claims that computer programs and technology will become the center of organizational memory and the stabilizing force holding tomorrow's organizations together. Additionally, an MIS will hold together dispersed organizations that employ a vast pool of transient, specialized labor. Likewise, it has been asserted that "computer programs . . . are nonhuman organizational structures. They are composed of executive programs and open or closed routines which perform functions and relate to one another in ways analogous to the relationships among levels in human hierarchies" (Klahr & Leavitt, 1967). Thus, it is possible that organizational structures may become more closely modeled after the communications, information, and decision requirements of the organization, as represented by the MIS (Malcolm & Rowe, 1961). This represents a vast improvement over past methods of organizing. Structures have often been designed, not in accordance with a logical means of accomplishing the work, but in response to the absence of information. Frequently, overlapping or duplicating procedures were, and are, employed strictly as back-up systems for unreliable or failure-prone information systems (Drucker, 1967).

CENTRALIZATION-DECENTRALIZATION CONTROVERSY

The largest controversy surrounding the implications of MIS utilization for organizations is whether centralization or decentralization of structure will occur. The term organizational structure refers to "a set of roles and role relationships, . . . a set of ordered work flows" (Klahr & Leavitt, 1967), or, as Meyer (1968) puts it, "the arrangement of work by divisions or subunits and by levels of hierarchy, and the channels of communication that are available to employees." As to the meaning of centralization and decentralization, Simon (1954) offers what is perhaps the classic definition: "An administrative organization is centralized to the extent that decisions are made at relatively high levels in the organization; decentralized to the extent that discretion and authority to make important decisions are delegated by top management to lower levels of executive authority." Later, Zannetos (1965) proposes a definition relating to the objectives of the organization. He believes a "unit is decentralized absolutely, always of course within the overall objectives of the total organization, if and only if its index of overall objectives is qualitatively identical to those of its parent."

Burlingame (1961) characterizes organizational centralization as pertaining to the locus of certain types of decisions. In centralized organizations, decisions that can be arrived at by evaluating factual, objective phenomena tend to be delegated, while tight control is kept on subjective decisions governed by intangible considerations. Conversely, in decentralized organizations, fewer distinctions are made between these two types of decisions. Instead, responsibility for both tends to be assigned to the lowest level, where the information, the ability, and the knowledge to use it coexist. Emery (1971) also identifies differences between centralized and decentralized organizations. His emphasis, however, is on the source of information within the organization. Higher levels of the organization, he contends, are the primary sources of information in centralized organizations. Just the opposite occurs in decentralized organizations, where the lower levels generate a majority of the information.

Decentralization can also be described in terms of the type of relationship that exists between general managers and division managers. Decentralized organizations can be characterized by a general management orientation that does not closely supervise the work of divisional executives. Just the opposite is the situation in centralized organizations, where close supervision over divisional executives is maintained by general management (Haberstroh, 1961).

Finally, recognizing that the concept of centralization is very difficult to measure, Whisler (1964) proposes that the distribution of compensation within an organization be considered to reflect the distribution of control. He also assumes that the concentration of control can be equated with the organization's degree of centralization. Thus, by measuring the concentrations in the distribution of compensation, the extent of organizational centralization can be determined.

In a real-world environment, where firms have historically faced increasing complexity, the typical organizational response has been to grow much larger, more bureaucratic, and more specialized. Organizations have often been forced to become more decentralized in order to maintain control, flexibility, and speed when dealing with changes in their operational environment (Leavitt & Whisler, 1958; Stern, 1971). With the advent of MIS, however, the trend toward decentralization may be slowed, halted, or even reversed (Emery, 1971; Hoos, 1960; Leavitt & Whisler, 1958; Stern, 1971; Vergin, 1967; Whisler, 1965, 1970b; Zannetos, 1965; et al.). The MIS may provide the vast, complicated communications system that large enterprises need in order to recentralize. In the past, it was extremely difficult to design and maintain such complicated organizational communications systems. Hence, top management often relinquished control of decentralized operations in order to keep pace with advances in technology. They did this by delegating responsibility to those with better working knowledge of particular functions. But as MISs are introduced, the systems will drastically reduce the amount of time needed to receive feedback for evaluating decisions and estimates. The instantaneous information available to top management through an MIS will allow high-level decision makers again to exercise coordination and control. The system will eliminate decision areas where lower management has access to more working knowledge than top management has (Leavitt & Whisler, 1958; Stern, 1971).

If in fact organizations tend to become recentralized in response to MIS usage, how will they do so? As early as 1958, Leavitt and Whisler predict (1) consolidation of functionally and geographically separate activities; (2) automation of middle management's routine activities; and (3) a shift to upper management of innovating, planning, and creating functions. By processing information rapidly, MISs will allow top management to extend their thinking to a wider range of problems, in addition to extending their control over their subordinates' activities and decisions. MISs will also tend to reduce the number of levels within the organizational structure, and to initiate a regrouping of activities and centralizing of control and authority (Hoos, 1960; Whisler, 1970a; Whisler & Shultz, 1962).

Anshen (1960) agrees with Leavitt and Whisler (1958) that MISs will stimulate the recentralization of geographically dispersed decision centers. However, he does not agree that MISs will automate middle management out of its important role, instead, he says, by relieving these managers of repetitive decision making and its accompanying paper work, MISs will allow them more time for judgmental and creative tasks. The jobs of middle-level decision makers could become very similar to the jobs of top-level executives.

A distinction is made between two types of recentralization caused by MIS. "One type relates to the integration of specific function and affects primarily the internal organization of the company. The other involves regrouping of entire units of the operation and causes sweeping changes of the external structure as well" (Hoos, 1960). Similarly, Emery (1971) thinks that an MIS will allow an increase in the range of tasks for which a particular subunit is responsible. As a unit's scope of activity expands, the division or breakdown of the overall objectives of the organization need not be as fine. Thus, the number of subunits comprising the organization can be easily reduced, as each subunit's span of control increases.

Another aspect of MIS that may stimulate recentralization of organizational structures is the development of integrated data files and applications, such as inquiry systems and on-line, managerial, planning routines. Such applications would tend to eliminate duplication of data, thus streamlining the organization (Lucas, 1973).

Obviously, the impact of MISs will not be identical in every organization. Many variables are operating to accent, nullify, or even reverse these effects. For example, it is probable that organizational structure will largely determine how information technology is used. Therefore, if the structure indicates strong external pressures on organization, then the impact of an MIS will be limited. Economics is another factor governing the extent to which structure will be affected by MISs. Usually, technology is exploited to the extent that benefits and costs are equitable. Hence, as hardware and software improve and become cheaper, the cost/benefit ratio will change, with a consequent acceleration in the usage and impact of MIS within the organization (Whisler, 1970b).

Discussing organizational conditions that favor centralized structures, Zannetos (1965) cites three important factors: existence of consolidated overall goals; complementary resources and operations for achieving these goals; and interrelatedness of the production function of suboperations within the organization. He finds, too, that firms with comparatively short production lines and pronounced geographic centrality tend to be quickest to achieve integrated MISs (Taylor & Dean, 1966).

Some evidence of recentralization caused by MIS is cited in the literature. For the most part, however, such evidence is based on observations of organization charts, job descriptions, computer information systems, and interviews. For example, one study (Mann & Williams, 1960) is based on over 300 unstructured interviews collected over a period of five years from various managers of a power and light company. Discretion and control functions were shifting to a higher level, and the utility was becoming more centralized. It was found, too, that these changes were contrary to a strong company philosophy of participative management. Citing his findings as support for his and Leavitt's (1958) prediction that information technology would recentralize control in organizations, Whisler (1965) discusses the impact of the SAGE (Semi-automatic Ground Environment) system at NORAD (North American Air Defense Command). He finds that the command structure has shrunk from five to four levels and that the level of responsibility for controlling the use of certain weapons has shifted from the lowest level to what used to be the third level from the bottom. The results of a study (Hoos, 1960) of 19 business organizations that had introduced computer-based data processing seems to indicate that substantial changes had occurred in the structure of the organizations involved. Here, the consolidation of an information base and the development of programmed routines in the data processing department reduced the responsibilities of many of the other departments within the organizations. Thus the number of middle managers was reduced.

After interviewing managers of firms ranging in size from 89 to 23,000 employees, Vergin (1967) concludes that, as a result of computer usage, these firms experienced a recentralization of control over decision making. In addition, the data collecting and processing divisions tended to become more centralized. He does not, however, make note of any differences in the relationship between the size of the firms and the response to computerization. Another study, using unspecified methods of data collection, does find that the extent of centralization of the operations's function is greater in large banks than in small ones (O'Brien, 1968). Finally, Shaul's (1964) study makes all the more apparent the inconsistencies in the findings on effects of computerization. Looking at a variety of organizations, he concludes that the role of middle-level managers is not being diminished. In fact, these managers are becoming more important than ever in the computer age. Shaul also finds that the structure of the organizations studied has not changed significantly. This gives little support to the notion that greater organizational centralization occurs in response to computer usage.

After analyzing the impact of MISs on organizations, Coleman and Riley (1972) claim that several conditions must be met if an MIS is likely to cause organizational centralization. Not only must the system's information be available to top management, but top management must also make the decisions. As this is rarely the situation, they conclude that a properly designed MIS is more conducive to organizational decentralization than to its opposite. Similarly, despite the predictions of organizational recentralization (Burck, 1964a, 1964b; Leavitt & Whisler, 1958), Dearden (1967) declares that the increasing utilization of MISs will neither seriously affect top management's control of operations, nor positively generate a trend to recentralize organizational structure. Recentralization of structure or of the decision-making process might, however, have been accomplished by relocation of geographically dispersed decision centers, and not because the effort to decentralize managerial responsibilities had been abandoned (Anshen, 1960).

Regardless of the division of labor between computers and men, the hierarchical nature of organizations is very unlikely to change. As automation progresses, however, the ideal size of the units comprising the organization may continually vary. As a result, the question of whether to centralize or decentralize the decision-making process is recognized as one of the more prominent current issues in the area of organizational design. Just as there are those who think that centralization is the trend of the future, there are others who think just the opposite. It has been suggested, for example, that we really cannot choose either to centralize or decentralize organizations. Rather, the only viable course of action is to determine the degree to which organizations should be decentralized in response to computer-based information technology (Simon, 1960b). Fisch (1963) also asserts that computer technology will facilitate organizational decentralization and result in a wider span of management. Additionally, the possibility exists that the impact of an MIS may be manipulated (despite arguments to the contrary) to reinforce or strengthen a firm's philosophy of decentralization (Burlingame, 1961).

Dearden (1967) discusses two factors that necessitate delegation of decision making and authority, and thus have the effect of decentralizing the organization. First, top management has usually had time only for the most critical decisions. Second, even with identical information input, top management can seldom make decisions as effectively as experts who are close to the problem. Since the utilization of MISs will have little impact on the amount of time and level of expertise of top management, there should be no noticeable change (that is, recentralization) in large, complex, decentralized organizations. In fact, an MIS may increase decentralization by allowing top management to delegate even more decisions, because the system will provide them with a means to evaluate the performance of subordinates. However, this decentralization is not without its pitfalls. There is a greater chance that information will be distorted in decentralized organizations than in centralized ones because of the number of levels through which that information must pass (Malcolm & Rowe, 1961).

The distinction between decision making at the functional levels and control at the top administrative levels seems to have been blurred. For example, although an MIS may stimulate centralization of control to provide for effective direction, the need to maintain the potential for personal growth and motivation among employees may requre a decentralization of decision-making responsibilities. This can be accomplished by permitting top management to have a staff at the middle-management level, which has immediate access to operational data via the MIS. This staff could supply top management with detailed information regarding subordinates' performance (Rowe, 1962).

Recognizing this distinction between operations and control, a number of writers have expressed a view similar to Rowe's, regarding the differential impact of an MIS on functional activities and the authority structure. For example, Koontz (1959) points out that centralization of activities does not necessarily suggest centralization of authorities. Melitz (1961) mentions that computers will give organizations the ability to maintain decentralized management of operations and decision making, while at the same time enabling top management to accumulate central information for better control and policy formulation. According to Burck (1964a, 1964b), centralization of policy control and decentralization of operational authority are not inconsistent. Again, in the long run, the creative, managerial functions will be decentralized, while the operating functions of the machine will become centralized (Whisler, 1965). Similarly, Sanders (1969) stresses that information-processing activities may be centralized "without at the same time changing the existing degree of centralization or decentralization of authority." Likewise, decentralization of administration and centralization of communications may occur in unison (Dale, 1964). Lee (1967) also questions whether centralization, which occurs through integration of data within the system and standardization of the operating procedures it requires, will necessarily produce changes in organizational structure and consolidation of decision making. And Moravec (1965) recognizes that the time-sharing aspect of MIS can stimulate the centralization of system facilities, while at the same time allowing for decentralization of systems use.

Although it is not yet clear whether the impact of an MIS will stimulate organizational centralization or decentralization, it does appear that there are other forces at work to confound the situation. Because the controversy regarding the impact of MIS on organizational structures is far from resolved, it may be worthwhile to consider the situational factors that moderate or accentuate the interaction between computer technology and organizational structure. Many factors act to limit centralization: (1) limited memory capacity of the MIS; (2) legal restrictions in dealing with payrolls, tax deduction, and so on; (3) public relations difficulties; (4) past and current organizational philosophies; (5) geographic dispersion of the organization; and (6) political climate within the organization regarding centralization/decentralization. Also, because computer vendors may be paid differently, depending on whether they sell small systems to individual divisions of a company or one large integrated system to the home office, organizational structure may be influenced by salesmen's commissions (Dale, 1964). Besides geographic dispersion, product-line variety may also encourage decentralization. The diversity of knowledge needed in such organizations may dictate against consolidation of authority or control via the MIS (Zald, 1964).

The planning and designing of MISs have perhaps their greatest relative influence on the eventual effect of the system on organizational structure. Intentional funneling of information to top management for the purposes of decision making, or detailed review of subordinates' discretionary activity will accentuate the centralization of structure. Conversely, designing the system to disperse information to various levels in the organization with the intent of giving autonomy to the decision makers at these different levels will reinforce the decentralization of structure (Coleman & Riley, 1972; Lucas, 1973). The extent to which the organizational environment is competitive (Argyris, 1967), or is controlled by governmental regulations and restrictions may influence too the ultimate impact of MIS upon organizational structure.

Two additional factors that influence the relationship between organizational structure and computer technology are those of economic feasibility and social desirability (Albrook, 1967; Klahr & Leavitt, 1967). As mass production reduces the cost of computer technology, there should be an acceleration of usage along with a corresponding enhancement of impact on organizations. Another aspect to consider is the scarcity of financial resources. In austere conditions, centralization of organizations is accentuated by their ability to respond more quickly to environmental situations. Regarding the social desirability of MIS, the issue of man-machine interaction may in fact be reduced to the nature of interaction between man and man, as mediated by the new computer technology. Haberstroh (1961) indicates that environmental pressures, which threaten a collapse of the traditional ways of doing things, may stimulate planning and change. Therefore, when examining organizational responses to MIS, extrinsic stresses upon the organization should not be overlooked.

Several societal forces, as discussed by Whisler (1965), encourage the trend to decentralize the structure of control in organizations. The mobility of the work force, the value placed on education, and the importance given to research and development may all act to lessen any centralizing effect. This is so since mobile, professional workers often prefer to relate to one another on an equal basis. Also, their flexibility and mobility may tend to loosen the strict definition of jobs, which has been common in the past, thus slowing any centralizing influence of the computer. Another factor is management's tendency to retain a decentralized structure as a training ground for future top management. It seems that centralized organizations are not considered as valuable as decentralized structures for providing the diversity of experience necessary to develop top quality managers (Leavitt & Whisler, 1958).

The impact of MISs on organizational structure also depends on the organization's size. For example, given some modification due to MIS, such as a reduction in the number of middle managers, the effect of this modification will be proportionally less upon a small firm. This appears to be due to the greater number of workers and more numerous communication channels present in large organizations. With organizational size, and all the other factors possibly confusing the issue, it is not surprising that considerable disagreement exists as to whether decentralization or recentralization of structure will be the major response of organizations to the introduction of MISs.

CONTROL AND POWER STRUCTURES

Certain characteristics of MISs will probably influence organizational form. One prominent feature of MIS concerns its effect on control (Porter & Mulvihill, 1965). Several assumptions underlie the emphasis placed on control, as engendered by MIS utilization. First, it is usually taken for granted that more sophisticated uses will be developed for future MISs (Sanders, 1969). Second, no end is seen to the exponential increase in data that management must handle (Vandell, 1970). Consequently, top managers in a position to utilize MIS could be convinced of the necessity to develop stricter planning and control.

There are those who stress that an MIS is only a subsystem of the control structure of an organization. Consequently, they say, control must be considered in designing, implementing, and using information systems (Ackoff, 1967). In order to this effectively, however, some practical means of evaluating management control systems is needed. Such a means may exist in the form of simulation models used in conjunction with standards for judging performance. A simulation scheme of this type should be primarily concerned with the control, information, and decision facets of management. Also, such simulation capability should provide management with answers to "what if" questions, thus giving decision makers greater control (Malcolm & Rowe, 1961). As Canter (1972) states, "the availability of accurate, reliable, comprehensive, and timely information in the hands of top management, and the ability of the computer to process data under predefined decision rules, will enable top management to control a greater part of the [organization]." Likewise, Ansoff (1965) stresses the potential for effective control that MIS offers future organizations. Thus, it is expected that top management will welcome MIS usage because of its implicit potential for allowing top-level decision makers additional control over middle management (Leavitt & Whisler, 1958).

The usual means by which managerial control has been achieved include "organizational planning, scheduling of operations, inventory control, quality control, [and] cost control" (Malcolm & Rowe, 1961). A major advantage of an MIS is its ability to unify or integrate these aspects of organizational operations into a single, unified control system. The extent to which this has been recognized and taken advantage of, however, is nowhere near its potential (Koontz, 1959; Malcolm & Rowe, 1961). MISs will also increase top management's control of middle management by providing greater administrative capability, by assisting in more accurate and realistic goal formulation, and by improving the evaluation of middle-level performance by helping to determine the variance attributed to environmental differences (Anshen, 1969; Dearden, 1967). Beckett (1965) also agrees that MISs will facilitate evaluation of the effectiveness with which the organization and its components perform. Another reason cited by Beckett for MIS's ability to improve control is that it may be used to signal the need for human decisions regarding management of planned activities that are not yet programmed into the system. By notifying management of the resources and the informative-feedback requirements of the organization, MISs will establish themselves as vital segments of the control process (Malcolm & Rowe, 1961).

Both Shaul and Whisler find some evidence of a systematic influence on control. The computer has been very important in providing top management with better control, and this has resulted in a loosening of the strict rules affecting middle management's decision-making authority (Shaul, 1964). Conversely, Whisler (1970a) finds that MIS capacity for better control results in tighter discipline on individual behavior at lower levels in the organization. These findings are somewhat confusing and hard to compare, and they may not be dealing with the same aspects of control. Thus, it has been recommended that future research in this area should be directed toward identifying the variables that competent managers are actually able to control (McFarland, 1971).

Several issues may arise concerning organizational control as influenced by MIS. One problem deals with the particular leadership style of top management. For example, in an organization that has communications difficulties, an MIS that provides data to all members of the organization could conflict with top management's strategy of keeping groups uninformed about each other and the total organization. Such a strategy might be used if top management felt it necessary to maintain firm control over the organization. On the other hand, the top management of another organization might desire an MIS that provides wide distribution of information, because it would reinforce their philosophy of leadership style and organizational behavior. Top management's implementation of, and reaction to, the MIS may thus be highly dependent on managerial style (Stern, 1972b). McGregor's (1974) theories of motivation are also relevant here. Theory X is associated with directive, controlling centralized leadership, Theory Y with participatory, delegating, decentralized leadership. Thus, under Theory X leadership, an MIS agreeable to top management would be associated with organizational centralization; under Theory Y leadership, an MIS agreeable to top management would be associated with organizational decentralization.

Another problem associated with MIS has to do with managerial motivation. In an organization where top management's control is being reinforced and centralization of structure is occurring, the motivation and performance of middle managers will suffer if the shift in control toward the top is perceived as threatening middle management's own authority and accountability. Such a reaction would naturally discourage middle management from contact with the MIS ("How the computer," 1967). If lower-level executives see themselves becoming weaker due to MIS use, while top management becomes stronger, more directive, and controlling, these threatened underlings may attempt to protect themselves by censoring or delaying the information they present to their superiors. That is, lower-level managers may tend to hide problems until they are able to offer a solution, thus reducing the pressure on them (Argyris,

1966a). This type of reaction, however, defeats top management's original purpose in using MIS to obtain more accurate and timely information with which to make decisions.

Another factor may also be limiting the impact of MIS on organizational control. It is likely that the methods used to obtain operational control within the organization are not useful for achieving effective managerial control, because of differences in information requirements. That is, management problems are not merely more complex and difficult operational problems. Rather, while operational activities can often be reported almost instantaneously by using MIS, higher-level management problems tend to be less structured and programmable. High-level decisions usually concern nonroutine situations, which are infrequent. Also, in such discretionary activity, speed of decision making is not as critical as it is in operational situations (Dearden, 1964). McFarland (1971) also stresses the slower time scale of top-level decisions. He believes that this slower response time makes the analysis of executive behavior, which is usally considered a continuous control process, extremely difficult. Finally, it has even been implied that, although MIS is excellent for communications, it is an appalling means for achieving control. Just as the telephone was a boon to individual communications but a poor instrument for exercising control, so MIS may be an aid to organizational communications but a poor means for obtaining better control (Reynolds, 1969).

Another aspect of control that bears scrutiny is span of control (SOC), "the scope of activities that can be centrally controlled by one controlling entity, be it man, machine, or combination of the two" (Carroll, 1967). It has been found, for example, that the technology of production is more important than organizational size in influencing the SOC of first-level managers (Walker, 1968). What effect does MIS have upon SOC? Rowe (1961) thinks that if an MIS causes decentralization, then the SOC would probably decrease, enabling people to be more closely supervised, and thus preventing mistakes and distortions in the transmission of information. Others have predicted that SOC will increase and eliminate the need for excessive middle managers. MIS's ability to use routine control procedures will reduce the requirement for supervision and communications between individuals, therefore aiding in the supervision of more than the traditional six or seven workers (Dale, 1964; Shaul, 1964; Uris, 1963a, 1963b). Finally, Meyer (1968), studying the changes in organizational divisions controlling the MIS, finds that the SOC tends to increase for first-line managers and decrease for higher-level managers. Again, it appears that additional research is needed to clarify what is actually happening.

An additional dimension of organizational structure that may be affected by MIS is that of delegation of authority (Krauss, 1970). Studying the implications of MISs for several organizations, Hofer (1970) notes that MIS made possible top-level management's delegation of authority to lower-level management without a loss of control. Authority is usually delegated to provide a more rapid organizational response to fluctuations in the internal environment. Such a shift in power shortens communications channels to important lower-level decision makers and gives them greater motivation and freedom in which to operate (Vandell, 1970). Sanders (1969) also emphasizes that adequate controls are needed if delegation of authority is to occur. Top-level executives are more prone to delegate decision-making responsibilities when they are certain that the transferred power will not be misused. An MIS will allow them to determine if a subordinate's performance deviates from acceptable standards: thus they maintain, and even enhance, their control.

It is frequently said that information is a source of power. The notion of organizational control is closely related to the concept of power: control may be considered the expression of power; conversely, "power necessitates control" (Sage, 1968). An MIS is often perceived as a key to power. Such a system can be used as an instrument of personal power by any executive who is able to control the flow of critically important information (Field, 1970). Frequently, conflicts and struggles develop within an organization regarding the control of, and the responsibility for, an MIS, because such control is seen as vital in determining the distribution of power within the organization (Kraut, 1962; Mann & Williams, 1960; McFarland, 1971). McFarland suggests that it may be possible for someone to usurp power from top management without their knowledge by cleverly using or misusing an organizations' MIS.

The concern with MIS as a source of power is also related to the leadership style of top management. An autocratic top-level leader will likely use the MIS to strengthen his organizational control and power. Conversely, a more democratic top-level executive will not be as dominating in his management of the MIS (Neel, 1971). Particular problems may develop within organizations, especially smaller ones, in response to a top-level manager who uses the MIS to solidify and strengthen his position and power. In an attempt to retain power and control, this type of executive tends to delegate responsibility without authority. Such actions on the part of top managers make it difficult for the organization to retain competent middle-level personnel, who tend to leave the organization when given responsibility without commensurate authority (West, (1975).

It has been said that MIS utilization will make future organizations less dependent on traditional, formal, and coercive power. Instead, greater emphasis and influence will be accorded management on the basis of competence and knowledge. This shift will not only limit the arbitrary use of power, but will also change the structure of organizations. In the quickly responding, adaptive organizations of the future, MISs will deemphasize the relationship between superior and subordinate, and emphasize the relationship between peers. These working "partners" will be organized around the need for pertinent information. This portends more extensive usage of a matrix, or project-team, form of organization. A matrix structure is designed around relevant information rather than formal power. Usually, each member in a matrix group is given equal responsibility and authority with which to solve a particular problem (Argyris, 1966a, 1971; Radford, 1973). Reif (1968) reports what may be the beginning of this trend. He sees a shift in decision-making power from line to staff groups. This is accomplished not by giving staff more formal authority, but by giving them a greater participatory role in the decision-making process.

Several problems may occur, however, if competence and knowledge, instead of formal authority, become the foundation for power. Executives who previously operated with incomplete information but had the formal power to direct the organization may be threatened by the shifting emphasis to technical expertise as the basis for power. Managers who tend to control situations by withholding important information may also be threatened by MIS usage, which demands of them the disclosure of critical facts. This will change "the rules of the game" for executives who tend to manipulate others in order to achieve selfish goals. Also, the increased reliance on system information will likely make such decision makers feel somewhat less essential and powerful (Argyris, 1971; Vazsonyi, 1974). Thus, the shift from power and arbitrariness to competence and explicitness may require a different type of executive to function within the sophisticated organizational environment created by MIS technology.

ORGANIZATION OF THE COMPUTERIZED INFORMATION DEPARTMENT

In addition to the general implications which MISs have for organizational behavior, the specific problems regarding how to organize computer systems within the firm must also be considered. Such aspects as the internal structure of the department responsible for the computer system, the location of the MIS department within the organization, and the status of the system's management, are all important facets of the organization's response to MIS usage (Brabb & Hutchins, 1963; Daniel, 1961).

Historically, as organizations first began to make use of computer technology, such use was primarily in the form of electronic data processing (EDP). Therefore, the EDP function was usually dropped into the existing organizational structure under the control of the accounting, financial, or controller's department (Porter & Mulvihill, 1965; Slater, 1967). As a result, it was nearest the usual sources "for most of the information to be processed, . . . in a department familiar with processing data, and . . . in the department that should be most familiar with serving the needs of company managers" (Koontz, 1959). As computer applications advanced from the highly routine and structured tasks of EDP to the more sophisticated integrated information and programmed decision-making routines of MIS, problems developed regarding the proper organizational locale of the MIS. That is, how should an MIS department be structured, who should have responsibility for it, and where should it be located within the organization in order to optimize the system's efficiency in servicing the total organization (Churchill, Kempster & Uretsky, 1969; Dickson, 1968)?

There is some indication that the efficiency of the MIS function will improve with the centralization of the information processing department (Albaum, 1964; "An overview of," 1969; Dearden, 1967; Meyer, 1968). Consequently, most organizations are following this method. For example, Meyer finds that the departments responsible for the computer system in a large number of firms had more levels of hierarchy, a wider span of control for first-line supervisors, and a narrower span of control for higher-level managers, than other divisions within these same organizations. Garrity (1963) also finds that computer systems departments are tending to become centrally organized, even in instances when the organization as a whole was decentralized.

In attempting to optimize an MIS's organizational effectiveness, top management should not overlook the problem of finding the best locus of control and responsibility for the MIS department (Gibson & Nolan, 1974; Kegerries, 1971; Whisler, 1965). The alternatives are few: (1) sharing responsibility with all departments of the organization; (2) giving responsibility to an existing major department, such as the accounting department; (3) creating a new independent department to administer the system; and (4) retaining responsibility within top management (Brabb & Hutchins, 1963; Neuschel, 1960). A large number of management scientists and organizational researchers prefer the latter two choices.

Among those who emphasize the importance of top management's retention of the responsibility for MIS are Brabb and Hutchins (1963), Churchill, Kempster, and Uretsky (1969), Garrity (1963), Gibson and Nolan (1974), Mumford and Ward (1966), and Schoderbek and Babcock (1971). As information technology can influence the strategy and structure of the entire organization, top management's direction and control are needed to minimize the potential conflicts and problems associated with MIS usage. Top executives, therefore, should assume the responsibility for the MIS function.

As to the location and nature of the information system's department within the organization, the consensus of opinion favors the establishment of an entirely independent information systems group. This unit should be directed by a specialist in computer and information systems, who reports directly to top management. In this way, the information systems department will experience less pressure from the operating groups it serves (Dale, 1964; "How the computer," 1967; Kegerries, 1971; Mumford & Ward, 1966; Poindexter, 1969; Schoderbek, 1971; Schoderbek & Babcock, 1971). There are many advantages to this arrangement. The department controlling the MIS will be able to meet the short-term operating requirements of other departments, and at the same time have the independence necessary to develop broad, long-term, organizational applications without undue interference from the operating department. Also, the staff of such an MIS group may be selected according to specific knowledge of MIS technology, techniques, and requirements. This staff will have a much broader perspective of the total organization than the operating executives whose first concerns are their own particular departments (Mumford & Ward, 1966; Schoderbek & Babcock, 1971).

Locating the information system effort in an independent department is not without certain disadvantages. For example, while the staff of such a unit may have considerable expertise in computer and information technology, they may possess less than complete understanding of the needs and operations of the other departments comprising the organizations. Also, operating executives may at times perceive the actions of the MIS group as intruding on their own power and authority (Schoderbek & Babock, 1971). Nonetheless, an organization's MIS will be most effective when located in an independent department, able to serve all parts of the organization on an equal basis.

A significant problem exists with regard to the operational definition of that organizational executive who is responsible for the computerized information system in toto. Each author reviewed has a somewhat different perception of this manager, his proper title, and locus within the organizational structure. A generalized job analysis attributes the following tasks to this executive: management of "the joint efforts of system analysis, system design, computer manufacturing, computer programming, and system training" (Malcolm & Rowe, 1961). Although this general job description elicits few debates, the name or title attached to it varies considerably. This variance confounds discussion; in order to avoid confusion, we will assume that this executive holds the title "MIS Manager."

Solving the issue of the position's title was very simple when the problem of proper or most efficient placement within the organization was considered. Leavitt and Whisler (1958) conjecture that even though the location of these managers is nebulous, they should ultimately assume a position near the top. According to Anshen (1961), they will "occupy a position of growing significance in the organization and will have an increasing influence on the whole system of information processing and decision making." However, they will not be allowed to assume top-level responsibilities and they are not likely to represent a potential pool from which top-management personnel may be drawn. As Vergin (1967) suggests, this top-level position is attained through assumption and subsequent delegation of responsibility and authority. He indicates that originally the MIS manager was on "an obscure low-level" within the organizational structure.

The manager's locus within the organization structure has been equated with the measure of an MIS's ultimate success (Garrity, 1963). Garrity seems to think that if the executive is placed high enough, the MIS will succeed. Of equal importance is the need for top management's active participation and leadership. Schoderbek (1971) similarly argues that the status of this manager and his personnel must be lucidly defined by top management. The MIS manager should be an "independent member of the top management team." Rader (1968) predicts that the system will be controlled by a corporate-level manager. Taylor and Dean (1966) suggest that within a centralized structure, the MIS manager will be located at the main office with line responsibilities. In comparison, the decentralized organization will favor "a staff executive," also in the central office, who possesses a mandate from top management to see that the systems groups are efficiently coordinated. Later, Dean (1968) discusses "the emergence of the top computer executive (TCE)." The TCE will be placed at the corporate level, presumably near the top, and, according to Dean, will absolutely require considerable power. Unlike Dean, Barnett (1969) suggests establishing an exact position: "executive vice president of information systems." This position would be "second-only-to-the-president." Gibson and Nolan (1974), discussing their four stages of MIS growth, identify the fourth and last stage as that point when the "MIS manager has [finally] broken into the ranks of senior management, having risen to the level of vice president or equivalent thereof." Similarly, Hanold (1968) summarizes the placement problem in terms of the computer department's growth. He expects status change to occur over a ten-year period. Originally, the head of the electronic data processing group was subordinate to the head of the systems department who was responsible to the assistant controller. Now, the head of the department will be a "corporate vice president" of information systems.

As the MIS pervades organizational functions and operations, it becomes extremely important to foster the growth of cooperative relationships between the technical-type manager and his functional peers. Effective and efficient management of the MIS effort involves the intimate linking of the system "with the activities to which it is applied" (Taylor & Dean, 1966). This coupling is greatly dependent on managerial cooperation. Organizations have tended to adjust their activities to optimize this cooperation. They have been placing operating people in charge of MISs, assuming that it will be easier to verse functional managers in systems technology than to educate systems types in business procedures. Brabb and Hutchins (1963) do not see this attitude carried through to members of these dichotomized organizational units. As opposed to Taylor and Dean, they believe it is better to teach the programmer about accounting than to attempt to educate the accountant in programming techniques. As Barnett (1969) describes, either method will create a "knowledge gap." The MIS manager will not understand the functional executive's problems, and the functional manager will not understand the problems of the executive. Jayant (1974) seems to feel that this gap has been perpetuated by the MIS manager. "The walls of specialization" that surround their creator, the MIS man, are responsible for this situation. Jayant suggests that the failure of MIS managers to receive development program opportunities that could assist in the absorption of these executives into the culture of the organization is the result of continued structured isolation. Operational-type managers see the MIS as being designed behind "four walls of a closed room, with little or no testing of the 'real world' in which the decision-makers lived and operated" (Horton, 1974). The rejoinder of MIS executives is that the functional-type managers "don't know what they want anyway," so in essence they have assumed the job of design despite its difficulties. There are no easy or concrete rules for solving this tradeoff. One potential solution requires that quality of communication between MIS management and top management, as well as between user and MIS personnel, be improved (Gibson & Nolan, 1974).

A corollary problem to that of MIS/functional manager relationships is what Hoos (1960) describes as " a strong tendency towards empire building" by the MIS executives. Hoos thinks that as MIS applications expand throughout the organization, the functional responsibilities of other departments will be undercut and top management's authority will be truncated. Berkwitt (1971), on the other hand, feels that top management "encouraged elitism," and as a result had "spawned a monster it cannot control." He claims that few top managers knew anything about the operations of their MISs. MIS managers lack curiosity, and have maintained their status and elitism "by making a fetish of being isolated and obscure." Yaffa and Hines (1969) describe MIS managers as being involved in a power struggle, which is directed at taking over the control or authority of the traditional manager. The computer-type managers "have had too much responsibility for information systems, and operating managers too little" (Thurston, 1962). This "unexpected abdication" by management, and subsequent usurpation by the MIS team, is directly related to the amount of change occurring in the department—and in the organization (Vergin, 1967). Gibson and Nolan (1974) indicate that, in fact, top management's support of the MIS group has placed "the MIS manager in a position to legislate policies internally that will exploit the computer as fully as possible," and potentially initiate organizational modifications and alterations.

Argyris (1971) and Field (1970) do not entirely agree. As indicated by Field, MIS managers have been held in awe and disdain by line executives. Field suggests that, although the MIS manager occupies a revered, yet ill-defined position, he is still divorced from the primary center of organizational power. Like the computer itself, MIS managers are hired before they are needed or understood, and thus are underutilized and/or "misutilized." As mentioned earlier, this group of specialized managers is isolated and insulated by "their abilities and their mystique." However, as Field suggests, this walling-in inhibits communication and may cause these managers to be ignored, by-passed, or allowed trivial participation. MIS managers "yield too easily to pressures from line managers and produce several outputs which become redundant in a short time" (Jayant, 1974). This is a far cry from the powerful status/elitism described previously. Argyris affirms that organizational politics hamper the whole system. Functional managers either provide irrelevant information to the MIS department, or fail to adhere to MIS-made decisions. Argyris suggests that the sophistication of the MIS will tend to circumvent politics by following the systems approach to managing the entire information network. Again, the MIS manager is not the all-powerful information dictator implied in the previous paragraph. It should be noted that, whatever the posture assumed by the MIS manager, the ramifications are necessarily important to the organization.

Another crucial element is the effect the MIS manager's skills and abilities will have on job performance. Keller (1966) describes the MIS manager's job as involving "round-the-clock 'fire fighting' . . . a result of haphazard scheduling." Ineffective scheduling has resulted from inadequate control of the incoming work flow. It does very little good to efficiently schedule computer operations if there is not similar control over the demand for time. Ransdell (1975) suggests that the MIS manager's track record of missed schedules for projects is actually a consequence of the generally accepted assumption that managing a system is a hit or miss proposition. Alexander ("An overview of," 1969) says that expansion of MIS applications imposes a new requirement on MIS managers. They must "become as skilled in the problem side of the ledger as they now are in the process side." Jayant (1974) agrees that the MIS manager's involvement in the decision-making process is essential for the acquisition of insight into the information needs of the decision makers. Another job restriction inherent to the MIS manager's position is the high degree to which procedures are formalized. Any "random policy change" made by this executive could disrupt the entire system. Therefore, the degree of discretion an MIS manager may work with is extremely small. The skills and tasks requirements of this technical job tend to be prescribed by the organizational environment.

6
EFFECTS OF COMPUTER-BASED MANAGEMENT INFORMATION SYSTEMS ON ORGANIZATIONAL PROCESSES

ORGANIZATIONAL CHANGE INDUCED BY THESE SYSTEMS

Revolutions, silent and gradual, often continue to go unnoticed long after their birth. It is these "quiet revolutions" that usually cause the greatest impact on people. The fact is, quiet revolutions have been the foundation from which many of the other more noisy and speedy revolutions have grown. According to Boettinger (1969), this is true regarding the impact of technological innovations. Organizationally, the technological revolution has taken many forms, one of which is the use of MISs. An organization's MIS has become increasingly "part and parcel" of its total resource foundation (Murdick & Ross, 1972). Technologically new information systems introduce major challenges to both the organization's capacity to alter itself and management's ability to cope with these systems (Kraut, 1962).

With a slightly different emphasis, Krauss (1970) states that it is evolution, not revolution, that as a philosophy is giving the MIS a new meaning and relevance. He tends to take issue with the name attached to MIS-initiated alterations, not with the fact that MIS requires an organizational "commitment to constant change." In essence, Krauss agrees with Boettinger, Kraut, Murdick, and Ross, and Whisler that organizational changes (evolutionary or revolutionary in form) take place when MISs are introduced, implemented, and utilized. According to Whisler (1970b) many forces within an organization cause change, but in the age of MIS, "technology often turns out to be a chief troublemaker." As Daniel (1966) states, technological developments such as MIS require organizational rearrangement in order that improvements in corporate performance may ultimately be realized. Stern (1971a) admits that the installation and implementation of a new MIS "is not a meaningful event unless it causes a change." In short, MISs force organizations to change: it is as basic and simple as that (Stern, 1971c).

Assuming this is true, the successful introduction, implementation, and utilization of an MIS require a fundamental understanding of Benne's and Birnbaum's (1969) "principles of changing." Some authors (Rogers & Shoemaker, 1971; Stern, 1971a; Vazsonyi, 1973d; and Whisler, 1970b) claim that a "change agent" is necessary for planning and implementing organizational change. This agent, who influences and introduces innovation into the organization, can be either an individual (as Rogers and Shoemaker, Vazsonyi, and Whisler assert), or a group of systems people (as Stern thinks). In any case, where the MIS presents a new and unique innovation, the skill and expertise of such a change agent is critical to organizational development.

Principles of change set forth axioms of alteration that should be heeded when MISs are introduced into the organization. According to Henne and Birnbaum, these principles are as follows:

1. To change a component of a system, relevant aspects of other components and the whole must also be changed.
2. To change behavior of any level of an organization complementary and reinforcing changes must be made on other levels.
3. The place to begin change is at those points of a system where some stress and strain exists.
4. Both formal and informal organizations must be considered in the planning of change.
5. Effectiveness of a change is related to the degree to which members take part in the planning and implementing of change. (p. 328)

The systemic nature of change becomes readily apparent in the above principles. Without adequate consideration of the interrelated, interactive character of MIS-initiated change, no organization will be completely effective in identifying all the advantages and disadvantages of such a system (Vergin & Grimes, 1964). Vergin and Grimes argue that foresight into potential organizational transformations, even with a systemic orientation, may be nearly impossible, because the uniqueness of each structure prohibits a universal posture to MIS-induced change. They also imply that the change agent (whether an individual or a group) is handicapped by rationally generated misconceptions of automation's impact and by a void in sufficient criteria upon which MIS effects can be evaluated. These misconceptions were created when the effects of factory automation were "logically" expanded to encompass the potential impact of an MIS on the entire organization. Criteria problems were, in part, caused by universal lack of expertise in both the application and use of computers by the change agent. It seems that the uniqueness of any organization, and the inherent complexity of MIS-initiated transformations, would motivate the change agent to devise a set of strategies for effecting modifications of the organization for MIS utilization. Such a set of "strategies for change" were enumerated by Whisler (1970b). These strategies are in general of three types:

> 1. The rational/bureaucratic strategy, with maps and blueprints made by experts and implemented using managerial authority.
> 2. Participative or human relations strategy, with all those who will be or think they will be affected involved in the planning, and action taken voluntarily by the individuals involved in the planning.
> 3. The cultural change strategy, with overall blueprinting done by a planning elite and action taken by appropriate operating units with the help of a key go-between person, the county agent. (p. 107)

Before a strategy can be chosen, the agent must answer the three major questions in organizational change—"when, what and how." According to Whisler, the question of when to change involves long-range organizational forecasts, plans and strategies. Deciding what to change necessitates a knowledge and understanding of the processes and relationships of an organization. This problem becomes complicated when the change agent has an inadequate knowledge of the essential organizational variables and their resulting relationships. Whisler, here, augments some of the concepts developed earlier by Vergin and Grimes, concerning potential difficulties in organizational change. It would seem that a change agent's organizational acumen may prove to be the most crucial element in the successful implementation of MIS-initiated change. The third problem, "how to get where we want to go," asks "what should be changed first and what later ?" and how can the company "be kept running while the systems are being installed ?" Technically, it is highly unlikely that a consensus of opinion concerning the proper solution to this problem could ever be reached. Whisler argues that motivating certain members within the organization to alter their behavior in the correct manner and at the proper time may prove very difficult. With these three basic questions and all their constraining conditions, the change agent must determine which strategy will best suit the specific situation. It is the skilled integration of these questions, and the chosen strategy of change, that will most likely result in a prosperous implementation. As Whisler points out, if the change agent fails to integrate properly, then an extended time span involving conflicts and adversities could be expected within the organization.

Another view of MIS-stimulated organizational change has developed around the idea that transformations will occur in phases (Gibson & Nolan, 1974; Mann & Williams, 1960). Mann and Williams classify organizational response to MIS implementation as a sequence of seven phases, as follows:

> (1) relative stability and equilibrium before change, (2) preliminary planning, (3) detailed preparation, (4) installation and testing, (5) conversion, (6) stabilization, and (7) new equilibrium after the change. (p. 221).

In this model, only the second through the fifth phases actually involve organizational change. It is in these phases that Mann and Williams find "extensive transfers of functions and employees," as well as significant reorganizations.

Gibson and Nolan have developed a four-stage organizational change model to explain the impact of MIS. Nominally, these stages are the following: (1) initiation, (2) expansion, (3) formalization, and (4) maturity. Gibson and Nolan are followers of the evolutionary doctrine discussed at the beginning of this chapter: their four stages of growth result from the evolution of MIS, not from any revolutionary change. They state that the division of MIS growth into four stages makes it "possible to sort out the affairs of [each] department, if not into four neat, sequential packages, at least into four relatively small, sequential cans of worms." Gibson and Nolan investigate the evolutionary changes that would occur in three areas: operational applications, personnel specializations, and managerial techniques. In the sections that follow, we will discuss both the personnel related alterations and the managerial changes that occur on an organizational level. However, before proceeding to these sections, we must discuss in general terms the effects of change on the individual.

The introduction of change into an organization is part science and part art. The scientific segment requires technical knowledge. The art, in contrast, involves the human resources affected by the alteration. As Williams (1971) asserts, the process of introducing change, making it agreeable to the human element, and attaining the requirements defined by the system or change is, "if not an art, . . . certainly an inexact science." Brabb and Hutchins (1963) conclude that "the degree and speed of progress in MISs will be defined by individual and economic conditions instead of technical considerations." Personal considerations arise when, for one of many reasons, managers and/or employees begin to behave in a matter not conducive to organizational change. Williams summarizes these difficulties and concludes that the basic problem is the organization's failure to reflect the human element. Haberstroh (1961) admits that the lack of consideration given to organizational members may be due to "the magnificent degree of flexibility for which human beings and organizations of human beings are well known." And he continues: "if people and organizations are adaptable, they are also rigid. If change and new patterns can be imposed, they can also be resisted."

Resistance to change is not a novel organizational problem. However, the introduction of MISs have added a new dimension to it. Elliot (1958) finds that employees resist because they may be required to learn new jobs, and they may be forced to work with new bosses. Resistance comes not only from employees. Williams (1971) claims that middle-level managers offer more resistance to alterations than do the subordinates who report to them. The "whole concept of resistance to change can be recoded as a problem of attitudes," he says; and he notes that "probably the poorest attitudes . . . come from managers, not other employees." Coleman and Riley (1972) also observe that change caused by MIS creates conflict and stress, which in turn make for resistance. They assert that resistance arises from a variety of factors: exterior fear that results from inaccurate perceptions concerning the system's ultimate effect; fear of the system as representing the unknown; threat to economic stability; anxiety arising from definable and enlarged responsibility created by the system; threat to organizational position and stature; and disruption of personal interrelationships due to system usage. Petroff (1973) agrees, and he adds to this list a fear of easier performance evaluation due to MIS usage. But Petroff believes that the likely MIS user will not be the individual but the organizational unit. Haberstroh (1961) points to a number of studies that demonstrate a direct relationship between the stress experienced by organizational members and their corresponding willingness to change. He claims that "only under stresses uniformly regarded as serious by all relevant personnel" will innovative transformations occur. Of the authors who have addressed the problem of resistance, only Mayer (1971) finds that none existed in the implementation of a personnel-data system.

However, this must be qualified, since it only reflects the attitudes of union employees toward an exclusively personnel computer system. It would be presumptuous to assume that this lack of resistance can be universalized to include management and all MISs.

In order to circumvent the resistance issue, three techniques have been recommended: participation of those involved in the change; maintenance of open communications before, during, and after the change; a combination form in which a committee oversees the change and utilizes both free communications and participation (Coleman & Riley, 1972; Elliott, 1958; Koontz, 1959; Petroff, 1973; Vergin, 1967; Williams, 1971). Koontz insists that "ample publicity" is the best means of dealing with resistance to, or fear of, change. Elliott has found that employee resistance to the introduction of a system into the Detroit Edison Company was overcome by maintaining an open and free communications network. Elliott and Vergin stress that internal communications must be accompanied by a sense of involvement in the decision-making process. Likewise, Coleman and Riley argue that both managerial endorsement and participation should accompany open communications if resistance is to be minimized. They also admit that this support of formal and informal changes may not be enough, in which case economic or psychological guarantees may have to be given to the organizational members. This would aid future modifications, for, as Williams points out, the organization's human element tends to react to alterations by focusing on the handling of previous changes and their consequences. Thus, the success of past changes increases the probability that future change will be accepted.

Petroff is the only author to suggest the formation of a committee to deal with the implementation of change. He believes that dissatisfaction can be reduced and/or eliminated by a "steering committee" that encourages management involvement. The committee approach exemplified the group-change-agent idea presented earlier. It is this method of introducing change that utilizes the other techniques associated with successful and satisfying organizational transformations. Haberstroh (1961) identifies a committee-type group called "the task force," which assists in introducing innovative change. Although this task force is not formed for the specific purpose of reducing resistance and other human-related organization problems, its very existence assists in doing just that. Haberstroh describes the task force as being a "small group which [is] expected to be disbanded upon completion" of the change. Its use has ultimately provided an excellent opportunity to train individuals for managerial positions.

A final note concerning the human element and change. "Apart from internal cost and attitudinal variables, company employee population size . . . [has been] reported to be the most influential factor in implementing" an MIS (Mayer, 1971). The notion here is that changes in the organization will ultimately result in increases or decreases in the member's population. Whisler (1965) argues the simple economic point that as systems become less expensive and more sophisticated in comparison to members or managers, substitution of one for the other begins. But, he says, "where to substitute and how much are the big questions." The organizational ramifications of this and other attitudes will be discussed in a later section. Suffice it to say that MIS-initiated change may produce alterations in the organization's membership.

The introduction and utilization of MISs cause major lags in an organization's progress. This slowdown in growth is especially noticeable during the introduction, or phasing-in, stage of an MIS. When the transfer of data among management levels in the organization's hierarchy is disrupted the consequences range from erratic forecasts and expensive lags in those programs the systems are supposed to assist, to the operational trauma of subordinate dissension over change (Berkwitt, 1966). After these problems are solved (or swept under the rug), some organizations reduce and restrict their MIS usage. Baum and Burack (1969) identify the low utilization to cost of system ratio as one of several explanations for reduced MIS operations. Among others are the hampering effect of old procedures on the new system, the extreme caution necessitated by radical procedural changes, and preoccupation by management with other company problems. Gibson and Nolan (1974) state that even if management decides to coordinate the entire MIS operation, the "dynamic force of expansion makes this a fairly difficult thing to do."

Although the literature contains considerable information on the problems associated with MISs, several authors (Mumford & Ward, 1966; Vergin, 1967) assert that very few studies have been undertaken, or completed, concerning the actual results of such a change. Mumford and Ward find that very little research has considered "the group most crucial to this kind of change; the programmers, system analysts, operational research experts and other computer technicians and technologists." Vergin affirms that "remarkably little evidence" has been gathered empirically. Another group of authors claims that MIS implementation has little or no impact on the organization (Baum & Burack, 1969; Hanold, 1968; Mann & Williams, 1960; Sanders, 1969; Vergin, 1967). Mann and Williams argue that, although MISs may have significant effects on one section of the organization, still other segments are not as immediately or extensively affected. As a result, broad statements concerning induced changes that drastically alter the organizational environment may need to be tempered. According to Vergin, the impact of MISs on the human element has not produced the resistance discussed earlier; in fact very little has changed. However, Vergin qualifies this by claiming that the published predictions were those of "academicians who have failed to perceive" all of the parameters involved. Sanders claims that the change potential of MISs is relative to application. That is, if the system is used to process "more or less routine" information, then a significant degree of change will not occur within the organization. According to Vergin, in organizations where MIS was installed to mimic simplistic tasks, the degree of change was practically nil. As such, organizational change may be directly related to the resultant application of the system. That is, change may or may not occur, depending on the MIS's eventual or prospective use.

ALTERATIONS IN JOBS, TASKS, AND FUNCTIONS

A brief definition of potentially ambiguous terms is essential here. Organizational jobs are said to consist of a set of related tasks. The firm defines the constraints of these tasks in terms of its goals and objectives (Klahr & Whisler, 1967). Thus, the structural makeup of a job can be defined as a cluster of tasks, each of which serves a specific function. This concept is essential for understanding the literature concerning the effects of MIS-induced changes on the jobs, functions, and tasks of employees.

Of particular interest are the alterations made by MIS, and projected and/or found to occur in job content. One study establishes that the procedures are simplified when certain operations are consolidated by MIS utilization. This simplification of work has the net result of enlarging related jobs (Elliott, 1958). Whisler (1970) indicates that this broadening of job content will probably be restricted to upper-management levels, and that clerical jobs will tend toward routinization and reduction in content. A correlative trend is discussed by Megginson (1963), who argues that "narrow and rigid" jobs are actually being expanded, and that the overall tendency has been away from specialization and toward generalization. This trend affects the managerial structure more readily than the supervisory or clerical levels. So it would seem that, as Shott and Albright (1963) suggest, clerical jobs are becoming more and more machine-like, with the system dictating task requirements. Vergin and Grimes (1964), however, assert that this mechanistic environment will improve working conditions through faster and more accurate information, thus ultimately improving the organizational member's jobs as well. But this job progression might occur only in situations of responsibility, for fast, accurate information would more readily assist the manager's job, especially in coordinating others' work (Lee, 1965). This may be why Lee finds that "managerial employees as a whole were relatively more content with the work conditions" after MIS installation than were the clerical employees. This author affirms that the reduction of "the employee's former freedom and flexibility in setting their own work methods," or job tasks, was the major cause of dissatisfaction. The literature implies that MISs will routinize jobs at a clerical level, enlarge them at the supervisory level, and could do either at the managerial level (Whisler, 1970a). Whatever the motive for installing an MIS, it is certain, according to Hoos (1960), that "all classes of jobs, from office clerk to vice president, are affected quantitatively and qualitatively."

If an MIS modifies the jobs in an organization, it necessarily alters the tasks that compose those jobs. Haberstroh (1961), discussing "the task model," indicates that the most crucial changes in these tasks have come about because of technological advances such as MIS. He states that task transformations will have organizational boundaries. That is, jobs, and therefore tasks, that are influenced by MIS utilization may be centralized in a single department or small cluster of departments, thus effectively limiting the scope of change. This structural restricting of task change is related to the point at which MIS enters the organization. Williams and Williams (1964) identify the management structure, rather than the organizational structure, as the hierarchy in which the primary impact of MIS is felt. They generalize that all of management will experience task modifications as a result of MIS implementation.

More specifically, Simon (1960a) predicts that by 1985 the following task clusters will be altered: eye-brain-hand coordination, MIS maintenance, and general management. He expects that the tasks normally requiring flexible eye-brain-hand coordination will diminish, and that the job of maintaining the MIS will require more and more attention. The tasks of general management will demand approximately the same energies as those expended currently. Delehanty (1966) concurs with Simon when he finds that the task requirements of technicians and systems staff have increased as a result of MIS utilization. He also notes that management's—in particular top management's—task duties have been expanded because of MIS. Ansoff (1965) disagrees with this. He believes that "the traditional staff activities of data acquisition, compilation, and presentation" will be usurped by the MIS. Unlike Delehanty, Ansoff argues that the tasks of staff members will effectively decrease with MIS usage.

In addition to modifications in task requirements, several authors (Anshen, 1960; Barnett, 1969; Delehanty, 1966; Diebold, 1969a; Ernst, 1970; Gibson & Nolan, 1974; Lee, 1967; Mann & Williams, 1960; Shaul, 1964; Walker, 1968; Whisler, 1970a) have discussed MIS-instigated alterations in the skill levels needed to satisfy the aforementioned task requirements. Anshen, Delehanty, Mann and Williams, as well as Shaul, agree that MIS has reduced the number of unskilled tasks and correspondingly increased the number of skilled tasks in those jobs affected by an MIS. Mann and Williams mention that typical high-level tasks involving minor decision making were eliminated, as well as routine low-skilled tasks. Whisler agrees, too: he says that skill changes are virtually omnipresent in the organization. However, he points out, the degree of transformation is hierarchically dependent. Clerical levels will experience the most change (a significant decrease in skill needs), while higher levels, sustaining an increase in task skill requirements, will see little, if any, modification. Gibson and Nolan state that successful utilization of MISs requires a management "strong in administrative skills." The tasks involved in developing and utilizing MISs are complex, and, as a result, have a higher skill requirement than those required at other levels. Thus, although the degree or magnitude of change is small, the skill requirements may be larger. Walker presupposes that the skill needs of managerial tasks will be modified, and that the resulting job requirements will have to be met through education. This, Walker indicates, "is based on the assumption that management skills can be isolated."

Training and education of organizational members in the skills needed to perform altered tasks have been thorny problems. Walker (1968), Ernst (1970), and Barnett (1969) emphasize training as a technique for upgrading the task-skill needs of managers, as well as lower-level employees. Each of these authors has a different view of who and what should be taught. Walker declares that education and training programs should give the manager a "knowledge and appreciation of the requirements" of the MIS. He argues that the task of decision making requires a basic technical understanding of the system, and he is joined in this stand by Barnett, who argues that "functional executives must be taught programming" together with an understanding of the limits of the computerized system. Barnett differs from Walker on the "who": he limits the training requirements to those managers who are responsible for specific functional areas within the organization. These functions are organizationally defined, and as such are somewhat unique to each structure. The idea is that skill development in MIS applications must come through the education of the managers in MIS capabilities and programming techniques. Ernst declares that besides the problems of education and retraining, there is a bias toward specialized training and experience as opposed to studies in the humanities. He infers that this bias has become an organizational necessity due to MIS usage. It is not just managers who will require training: there will also be "enormous requirements for analytical skills in business staffs." Thus, programs must be undertaken not only to train management, but to hire or retrain the staff.

Diebold (1969a) has found that when organizational members were asked questions concerning technical skill requirements for fulfilling their job responsibilities, 79 percent identified the skills of motivating and communicating as most important. This followed a similar study by Diebold who reports that a majority of the organization's staff and management "have not been successful in bridging the communication gap." Whisler (1970) identifies two areas in which communication skills have been altered: (1) interpersonal communications have diminished within clerical and supervisory levels due to MIS usage, and (2) interpersonal communications "chiefly at the managerial level" have increased because of a need for openness. Whisler qualifies this division, stating that skill requirements are dependent on the time span in which the MIS has operated. It is for this reason that clerical and supervisory levels have less need for interpersonnel communication skills. These groups have been working with automated information systems for longer periods than the upper-level managers. Thus, not only do MISs affect organizational jobs, related tasks, and required skills; they may also have an impact on the individual and his interpersonal relationships within the structure.

From the instant management begins to consider the feasibility of installing an MIS, "people problems begin to make themselves felt" (Kusher, 1963). According to Dickson (1968), "the manner in which MISs are introduced to an organization is obviously of critical importance to its acceptance, but again guidelines are absent to a large extent. Since all three levels of management information-decision systems . . . involve people as a component, knowledge of their behavior as a part of the system is important to the success of the entire field" (p. 24). In fact, individual problems in MIS implementation cause more disappointments and failures than do technical problems (Holmes, 1970; Megginson, 1963; Sackman, 1970). Personnel problems so difficult because they are not easily foreseen, and are usually not open to simple solutions. Evans and Hague (1962) claim that personnel problems have psychological, sociological, and philosophical implications. Megginson, in agreement, finds the origin of personnel problems in the "bipolar nature of man," which causes us "to desire to be treated as an individual while at the same time wanting to be accepted as part of a group."

This duality of needs inherently leads to frustration and anxiety, since creativity and individuality are reduced or eliminated by the MIS. Sackman claims that the magnitude of these human problems is greater than that of the problems associated with the MIS itself. Because personnel problems are not restricted to any specific point in an MIS's existence, Megginson, and Gibson and Nolan (1974) identify the introduction or conversion stage as that time when the very survival of the MIS is at stake. This crisis period places management in a position whereby failure to identify the seriousness of employee emotions lead to a more universal reaction. Gibson and Nolan describe the resulting personnel behavior as "unresponsive and uncreative"; extreme levels of uncertainty and anxiety might even culminate in sabotage. Managements have attempted falsely to reassure those involved that nothing will be altered in the employee's work. When the truth is unveiled and change does occur, the end result is a credibility gap with its notorious ability to resist closure. This environment spawns morale problems and a multitude of related difficulties (Megginson, 1963).

Koontz (1959), along with Mann and Williams (1960), describes the stresses placed upon nonsupervisory employees during the initiation of a computerized system; they include fear, low morale, anxiety due to uncertainty, disillusionment, and outward resistance. According to Holmes (1970), the lack of active participation by both the ultimate user and the related clerical staff may result in the system's failure. Evans and Hague (1962) suggest that employee resistance arises from a combination of factors, including fear of unemployment, perception of lost job security, and a feeling of inadequacy in performing the new job. Coupled with the influence exerted by the MIS itself, peer pressure directed toward employees who fail to "pull their share" increases with the implementation of MISs. Mann and Williams identify the ease with which failures can be detected and the fact that jobs are more interdependent as those elements contributing to this increase in employee-peer pressure. In addition, the MIS causes loss of employee esprit de corps: Conomikes (1967) predicts that "the 'dedicated employee' will become a vanishing breed."

When the job no longer presents the employee with an opportunity to satisfy his needs and aspirations, he will seek fulfillment of these desires off the job (Burlingame, 1961). MIS has forced this issue, creating a working environment that, according to Burlingame, is "devoid of intellectual satisfaction." In this environment, the employee "will attempt to curtail the freedom to act" of those he feels are pushing such conditions upon him. Thus, as said earlier, the individual becomes resistant to MIS introduction and utilization. He may blame the computer even for errors caused by other people (Conomikes, 1967).

Ernst (1970), discussing depersonalization within an organization, claims that the individual will perceive his role as an MIS-created niche that reflects only the requirements of the system, not the needs of the employee. Singly, the issues creating personnel depersonalization may be minor. But, as Ernst points out, clustered and accumulated, "they boost our frustration level alarmingly" and are seen as chipping away at one's individuality. An area of constant concern is depersonalization through invasion of privacy. Resentment may be created if the individual senses that his personal privacy has been, or may be, violated by the MIS or its users.

With the introduction of an MIS, "supervisors and older workers are likely to be especially hard hit" by the projected and/or actual changes in their organizational environment (Kraut, 1962). These individuals find it harder than do the younger employees to adapt to such changes. Ignizio and Shannon (1971) identify the "changing age profile"—that is, an increase in the young, educated worker—as a trend which will subtly replace older, less flexible, and staid employees with younger people who shun repetitive, undemanding work. Youthful workers tend to be more conformable with and desirous of change. As these younger, better educated, and less experienced personnel are introduced into the organization, an increase in the checks and balances of the management control system will be necessary. These requirements will have to be added to the MISs utilized, or thought to be utilized, by the organization. Kegerreis (1971) identifies this disparity between the ages of employees as a "generation gap." He believes that, because the MIS-type executives are "15-20 years younger than their organizational peers," the proverbial communication gap will be coupled with the generation gap, further complicating organizational behavior. Thus, claims Kegerreis, in addition to the age problems associated with lower-level employees, the organization's management must contend with the generation gap, or what was described by one executive as the firm's "most persistent high level sociopsychological problem."

Megginson (1963) and Meyer (1968) mention an ancillary problem of MIS introduction, namely, line-staff conflicts. Megginson states that the management of personnel is of greater importance after MIS implementation than it is before. Also, effective MIS operations require efficient staffs. The interrelationship of line and staff has become paramount for successful MIS utilization. Line-staff problems, as such, are more prevalent when functional managers interact with MIS staff experts. It is in this environment that we encounter the question, who actually possesses the final authority when disagreements arise? Meyer asserts that—as it has traditionally—the organization, with its vertical channels of communication, will force top-level managers to provide the required final decisions. Centralization of control, authoritarianism, and an atmosphere of inadequate personnel relations could result. Meyer suggests that in order to minimize both line-staff conflicts and the resultant question of ultimate authority, an MIS would have to enhance "horizontal interchange" so as to increase the level of cooperation between these two groups. No ideas or plans have been presented as to the means by which this can be done.

MISs assume a significant role in the repression of such organizational forces as "motives, drives, affections, . . . and levels of aspiration" (Field, 1970). However, Field also says that MISs repress "antagonisms" and "covert conflict." It would appear that although individual emotions were restrained, individual behavior within the organization was not. Problems with personnel interactions are not encouraged by MISs; on the contrary, says Field, MISs discourage them. One article ("People and machines," 1974) asserts that efficiency in an MIS can be realized through careful planning of man-machine interaction. This article recommends that implementation take into account the "interests, frustrations, capabilities, idiosyncrasies, emotional drives, and career aspirations of the individuals involved." Brill (1974) suggests a similar "cookbook" approach to avoiding or eliminating personnel troubles. He suggests educating both technical and line personnel in the mysteries of the system. Thus, career paths may begin to cross organizationally defined boundaries. In summary, Dickson (1968) states that for an organization to realize the technical benefits associated with MISs, the dysfunctional conduct of individuals working with the system must be minimized.

Many authors (Argyris, 1971; Burck, 1964a, 1964b; Gilman, 1966; Hill, 1966; Parsons, 1968; Simon, 1960a; Yaffa & Hines, 1969) do not share the doom and gloominess of the writers previously mentioned. In fact, according to Yaffa and Hines, "the predicted displacement and domination of people by the computer has not occurred." Simon disagrees with those authors who predict that MIS utilization will create stress; he believes that those kinds of interpersonal relations that cause stress will be reduced in importance when the organization begins to use the system. As a consequence, the organization will be happier or calmer. Similarly, Gilman states that an MIS "should reduce, rather than increase, the degree of impersonality in a large organization, since it eliminates the necessity for the practice that has led to impersonality." This directly conflicts with Ernst's (1970) notions, presented earlier. In fact, the projected demise of creativity, as discussed by Burlingame (1961) and Ernst, has not been realized. Parsons argues instead that the MIS will allow people to think freely. The system will give the individual time to exercise his intellect.

Organizational politics, although addressed directly by only one author, has the potential to cause many stressful situations. Argyris (1971) describes the tendency of department heads, as well as their subordinates, to "build walls" around their domains in order "to protect [themselves] from competing peers or arbitrary superiors." Environments such as the one just described can produce as many disruptive actions, both individual and organizational, as those attributed to MIS alone. Argyris, however, views the MIS as an asset, rather than a liability, with regard to intra- and inter-group politics. He claims that "a mature MIS reduces the need for organizational politics within but especially among departments. Discussing the radical alterations attributed to computerized information systems, Burck (1964a, 1964b) argues that even though the computer is the "bete noire of critics," the MIS is destined to emerge as a powerful tool through which organizations will become more creative and efficient. Not only will these systems eliminate the typical tedium involved in some organizations, but they will also contribute to "expanding free man's range of choices."

In addition to the attitudes concerning MIS-induced changes that we have already discussed, there are also perspectives from which alterations are seen in terms of the sociotechnical systems within the organization. Generally, the actions of the organization are considered a complex of social actions within a technical environment. In other words, the MIS can represent a technical subsystem of the organization, as the individual relationships can represent the social subsystem. The interaction of social and technical sybsystems indubitably creates problems. It is essential that existence of those factors that make MISs "socially unpalatable" be recognized and taken into account (Ernst, 1970). "As matters stand, a gross imbalance exists between technological and sociological progress. It is widening" (Karp, 1971). It would seem that the human element has found the transition to a technological society difficult.

Thompson (1961) expands the locus of technological impact to include the organization's hierarchy. In other words, he argues, in modern bureaucracies the combination of technological expertise and the "institution of hierarchy" has created an organizational pattern of conflict that has widened the gap between perceived technical requirements and authority. The intraorganizational conflicts alluded to by Thompson are similar to those political conflicts discussed by Argyris. An authority and/or power crisis will arise as the interdependency needed to operate efficiently in this technological environment increases. Higher-level executives may find that the sociotechnical environment in which their department operates has begun usurping their privacy and inhibiting the management of their organizational responsibilities (Baran, 1965; Gibson & Nolan, 1974). Gibson and Nolan assert that a "distinctive, informal organizational process [would] play an important role in giving rise to the issues which need to be resolved." These informal social structures, spawned as a consequence of technological advancement, could effectively negate any benefits an organization derived from the utilization of an MIS. Lipstreu (1960), reviewing the products of altered work environments due to technology, agrees with the previous writers. He suggests that "a new form of social organization" will be created in the plant. As do Gibson and Nolan, Lipstreu realizes that in order for an organization to attain its objectives, it must undertake a careful examination of the "social dimensions of work."

On a more individual level, "a complex interplay of human attitudes and values is involved in the information processing task" required of a worker in this sociotechnical environment (Anshen, 1960). Baran (1965) identifies the perception of lost privacy as one problem inherent to interaction with an MIS. The basic objection, according to Walker (1968), is that "no account has been taken of 'social success' as well as economic success—the extent to which a firm's organization was appropriate to its technology, in terms of the social satisfactions and dissatisfactions it provided." Similarly, Burlingame (1961) argues that organizational members must have pertinent facts if they are clearly to understand the relationship between their own and others' contributions and the best interests of the organization as a whole. He indicates, too, that advancing technology can contribute significantly to meeting the individual's work-related needs. However, close supervision is required to guide the system toward desirable results.

The ultimate impact of MISs on the jobs, tasks, skills, and individuals of an organization has been prophesied, prognosticated, projected, and pondered. Yet few empirical studies have been undertaken to identify and describe the actual effects of MIS use (Hill, 1966). Hill finds that "despite the abundance of information which has been generated, few conclusive statements can be made concerning the effects" of MIS because those involved have not clarified the salient components of the introduction and use of these systems.

CONSEQUENCES FOR EMPLOYMENT

If an organization introduces and utilizes an MIS, then what happens to employment? Will the absolute number of organizational members be altered? Will each hierarchical position be effected equally? Will the organization be required to alter its mix of line to staff employees? Or will there be no significant impact on employment? These questions have plagued both organizational management and members since the inception of MISs. As a result, a considerable amount of time and energy have been expended discussing, projecting, predicting, and in some cases investigating the influence of MIS on employment.

When the literature first appears on this subject, the consensus is that total employment will grow because of an increased need for people to handle the tremendous amount of information processed (Koontz, 1959; Stieber, 1957). Simon (1960a), however, demurs; he insists that "human employment will become smaller"—"relative to the total labor force." Internally, though, employment requirements will be determined relative to "comparative advantage"; employment needs will be based on a tradeoff between utilities. If the machine provides a better vehicle for obtaining organizational goals and objectives, then the human will be replaced and vice versa. Simon refines this doctrine to include the cost of tradeoffs, as well as the initial productivity measure. This reduces the theoretical possibility of an MIS eventually replacing (relative to productivity) all the members of the organization. In some form or other, Simon's thesis has been carried through the literature. Hill (1966) finds that the installation of a system has a mixed impact on employment: only "a small per cent" of the personnel are laid off as a direct result of the system, while most are either transferred or left completely alone. Vergin and Grimes (1964) suggest that the "degree of job reduction depends upon the previous state of mechanization." If a firm or department utilized a computer system prior to the installation of an MIS, the impact on employment will be only slight. However, Vergin and Grimes indicate that, under the opposite conditions (that is, lack of previous experience with mechanization), major changes will occur. Lee (1964) offers another important variable, time span, for consideration. Will the full impact of an MIS upon employment occur in the first couple of years or is the present phase transitional? He argues that in the future extensive manpower variations may occur. West (1975) summarizes the whole problem: "an MIS will fail if there are not enough competent people to do the job"—whatever the job may be. Thus, if MIS implementation and utilization cause a significant reduction in organizational employment, then the firm may no longer be capable of obtaining its stated objectives.

Let us presume that an organization's personnel ranks are diminished as a consequence of introducing an MIS. The next issue, then, is which group(s) of employees are affected and to what extent. Several authors (Hoos, 1960; Lee, 1964; Simon, 1960a; Vergin,

1967) single out clerical employees as that group most likely to feel the squeeze of MIS. It would seem, according to Hoos, that the traditional routines of clerical work are the most adaptable to MIS applications. Hoos says that "for every 5 office jobs eliminated, only 1 is created," and those that are not created or eliminated experience dramatic changes. Vergin suggests that the future impact of MIS will be exclusively constrained to clerical replacement. One group that has experienced tremendous growth is the key-punch operators. Hoos suggests that "these positions involve little, if any, upgrading" for the employees displaced by MIS. Lee finds that an MIS will indeed have "relatively greater" impact on clerical workers than on the managerial labor force. However, a few years later, Lee (1967) qualifies these and other findings on the effects of MIS on clerical workers: he now asserts that there has been no significant reduction in the number of clerical employees on the economy level and frequently no decreases in those individual companies affected. MIS, he says, has actually "slowed rather than reversed the rate of growth in clerical employment."

Weber (1959), in a study of two industrial firms, hypothesizes that the use of an MIS will require an increase in managerial manpower in comparison to the total requirements of the firm. Weber's data demonstrated that managerial manpower requirements will increase considerably during the transition, but will decrease as the system matures. Lee (1964) reports that Weber also found that the "proportion of managerial workers as compared to the proportion of clerical workers" would increase because of MIS utilization. Lee has conducted a longitudinal study of effects of MIS and found, in accordance with Weber's hypothesis, that managerial employment increases while both clerical and total employment decrease. Whisler and Schultz (1962) suggest that even though a greater number of clerical employees will be displaced, only about 20 percent of the total number of clerical workers will lose their jobs—compared to management, over one-third of whose members will be affected. But displacement, as such, is an all-inclusive effect: both internal and external movement are considered under that rubric. So, as Hill (1966) suggests, the organizational areas in which an MIS is introduced will experience a change in the ratio of managers to clerical workers that favors the former.

Of the possible personnel changes only one "seems to be more or less certain," that is, that "the installation [of an MIS] increases the number of staff positions, mostly technical" (Lee, 1967). Staff members with quantitative training will be increasingly necessary, and thus advance the cause and number of staff specialists (Ignizio & Shannon, 1971; Vandell, 1970). In order to maintain the organization's viability, as Vandell suggests, one "must build distinctive quantitative competencies." Vandell's thesis is that initially the central staff's activities "will mushroom," but ultimately technological knowledge will be maintained in the system's storage banks, as will "specific analytical procedures." However, in order to utilize these "stored resources" effectively, the "creative energies of the specialist" will be required. Murdick and Ross (1972) perceive a compounding problem in the organization's requirement for quantitative specialists—the "qualitative shortage" of these individuals. The demands for these sophisticated MISs must be met by better trained and qualified specialists than are employed today. Hoos (1960) suggests that middle-aged employees will find their years of experience no longer an asset. Involved in training periods of as long as a year, these older staff members may not make the transition. Vergin (1967) also discusses this organizational problem of obtaining and/or training technically proficient people. He says that the current shortage of qualified programmers has been compounded by a "rapid turnover and a high failure rate" among prospective programmers.

Ancillary to the staff specialist issue is the problem management encounters when attempting to organize and control individuals of diverse expertise. Gibson and Nolan (1974) conclude that "trying to introduce needed formalization of controls with the same personnel and the same organizational structure more often than not encourages conflict and the reinforcement of resistance rather than a resolution of the crisis" (p. 84). They suggested retaining "the experienced personnel who have the potential," and firing or laying off the others, opting to hire-on the highly sophisticated specialists. A Machiavellian attitude such as this could, and probably would, cause an employee reaction that is, to say the least, extremely counterproductive. Gibson and Nolan warn that in the early stages of MIS development, "the highly sophisticated professional should not be hired until his expertise is clearly required." If management, instead, assumes the position of insuring job security subsequent to MIS usage, the added staff requirements will produce an extensive placement problem rather than a selection problem (Mann & Williams, 1960). It appears that this managerial attitude will necessitate extensive retraining of current employees and thus require the virtually undivided attention of the coordinating managers. Dobelis (1972) implies that with all the problems surrounding the staff specialist, scheduling of these workers can create new difficulties. In essence, management has not realized that the MIS must be utilized 24 hours a day, six or seven days a week. Consequently, it has not informed the specialists that their working hours may not be short.

As with almost everything, there is a lot of disagreement about impact of MIS on organizational employment. Swart and Baldwin (1971), reviewing their survey results of MIS impact on clerical workers, conclude that there is "virtually no change." Uris (1963a, 1963b) indicates that "although a computer may replace some clerks, these jobs are often taken over by information technicians"; this results in a zero-sum game. Vergin and Grimes (1964) note that despite reductions in the number of jobs, MIS implementation "had almost no impact on the employment of the employees in the firm." They find that there are no substantial layoffs, because of organizationally anticipated reductions. Overtime and temporary help are used to meet its work requirements. Thus, the MIS has a greater impact on "employables" than it does on the employed.

INTERACTION BETWEEN THE SYSTEM AND ITS USERS

When an organization implements an MIS, a new set of interdepartmental interactions occurs. Gibson and Nolan (1974), as well as Poindexter (1969), have identified two forms of organizational orientation in response to MIS utilization. Poindexter describes how the two firms he studied assumed a user orientation. That is, individuals were assigned "to act as liaisons" for the information user to the MIS department in one firm, and in the other this role was reversed. Gibson and Nolan identify the other generalized orientation as MIS or technically directed. Rather than possessing an "understanding of or sympathy for the long-term needs of an organization," the individuals within the MIS department are professionally motivated: they prefer to tackle "technically challenging problems," and not organizational problems. What has happened—and what will happen—to organizations under one or both of these orientations?

One trend has been toward "user-oriented systems." The technicians and programmers provide the basic facility, but they do not meddle in the interactions between the user and the facility (Simon, 1967). Intraorganizational cooperation is the foundation of this orientation. Powers and Dickson (1973) find that users become extremely frustrated when they are bounced back and forth between programmers in their attempts to solve problem situations. However, when the organization provides a "liaison" between the MIS and the user, satisfaction and confidence in the system increase. With this positive psychological atmosphere, some users have developed a fascination with the system and its many applications. These individuals view the MIS as "a symbol of progressive management," or as a "status symbol for a department or individual." Fascination of this sort tends, however, to breed a form of enthusiasm not tempered by judgment (Gibson & Nolan, 1974). Couple the user's insatiable demand with the MIS technician's "euphoric urge to supply," an exponential growth will occur in the organization's budget. In such an environment, definite management constraint is essential for the maintenance of the organization. The payoff associated with a user-oriented system is a more efficient intraorganization-information system, provided that a strong management exists to temper the demands made of the MIS.

If the organization assumes a technical orientation or point of view, whereby the user is given second priority behind the system and its mentors, another set of internal problems is created. Hoos (1960) describes systems personnel with technical orientations as displaying "trained incapacity frequently bordering on artlessness, in its relations with other groups." In conjunction with the other group's awed perception of systems personnel in general, significant barriers to cooperative interaction arise. Bieneman (1972) suggests that the result of allowing MIS personnel to possess the power and responsibility for developing the system is to promote the "human tendency to guard one's domain," or, in other words, to "push their own ideas upon users" of the system. Bieneman says that system's personnel don't like being hindered by their conservative peers in the information-using departments. The users, on the other hand, hope to remain "uninvolved" with the MIS, and thus effectively avoid being considered for other systems "help." This user and MIS personnel parochialism will "erode the potential for the computer unit to act as an agent for innovation and change," presuming this posture is organizationally beneficial (Gibson & Nolan, 1974). Lacking clear management control over priorities, the result may be a sort of "wheeling and dealing" between MIS personnel and user groups with the organization ultimately being the overall loser.

The interrelationship of MIS department personnel and non-system managers has also been addressed in the literature. It seems that experiences similar to those the user meets with are occurring with the managers of these functional departments. Kleinschrod (1969) establishes that a "solid barrier between management people and [MIS] people" exists as a result of technicians speaking a language management fails to understand—computer language. Because of this basic communication failure, technicians have taken management's goal-setting responsibility for MIS applications upon themselves (Diebold, 1969a). Diebold demonstrates that this shirking and subsequent usurpation of goal-setting behavior is a primary reason why organizations fail to realize the true potential of their MIS investment. As Thurston (1962) states,

"Clear placing of responsibility for the control of information systems is one of the few ways in which top management can influence information systems work," although in most cases, control has gravitated "to the hands of the specialist," due to a lack of clear-cut decisions by top management and its "tacit" support of the technicians. Technicians, however, lack the understanding of organizational needs and opportunities in order to make objective goal-setting decisions. Nonetheless, Kleinschrod predicts that both the language barrier and managerial abdication will give way to management's assumption of its "proper role"—making essential decisions with regard to what the MIS should or should not do. Jayant (1974) also disagrees with Diegold when he describes the MIS man as accepting implicitly line management as the only group who understand the organization's objectives. Thus, he is the only one who can use "information for evaluating the performance of the function towards those goals." Some MIS personnel expect their jobs to cease once the information has been accepted by the manager/user. The other systems men have taken the attitude that, if they want their thoughts to be accepted and eventually implemented, then they must clearly define their organizational roles and functions, and develop skill in interpersonal relations (Mumford & Ward, 1966). It is unfortunate that none of these conditions usually exists. Jayant is also astonished to find few of the MIS personnel realize that this system, "placed in the hands of competent men, could change the whole direction and methodology of decision-making." Instead, systems people choose to stress the mystical nature of MIS, rather than the enormous potential that could evolve from the use of powerful computers.

The conflict and confusion caused as the number of MIS specialists grows and their degree of specialization increases "may be readily avoided if [these] specialists act merely as advisors to line management and carry no executive authority themselves" (Pettigrew, 1968). However, diametrically opposed to this view, Jayant (1974) suggests that in order to make the MIS effective, the system specialist should be rotated with the line managers. This will insure the integration of the system's staff into the organization, while simultaneously facilitating a basic understanding of the organization's objectives. To insure that the MIS staff specialists work toward organizational goals, management should utilize such human relations techniques as open organizational communications and should express an interest in the specialist's tasks (Coiner, 1973). The basic disagreement has not been settled. It seems that both points have some merit. In any case, the implicit assumption drawn from the literature is that the relationship of the MIS specialist to line management is, and should be, organizationally defined.

Programmers as a group have received disproportionate coverage in the literature compared to other related groups. Leavitt and Whisler (1958) describe programmers as one of two types of middle jobs that can move up through the organization toward "de-programmedness." Hoos (1960) identifies programmers as "the elite corps of the present office labor force," where opportunities are few, qualifications highly variable, and a great deal of exaggeration exists concerning actual salaries and potential for promotion. Vergin and Grimes (1964) suggest that although programmers will eventually be involved in managerial decision making, "it is difficult to forecast to what degree this [will] occur." Simon (1960a), however, dismisses the thesis that MIS programmers can become a powerful elite. He asserts that "it is far more likely that the programming occupation [will] become extinct." The belief that managers will eventually be replaced by programmers, or that managers will have to undergo extensive training in programming, was also discounted by Simon (1967). The only exception is that the programming requirement of systemic thinking will become a managerial necessity, as will the most important attribute of a successful information processor's logical aptitude (Nicholson, 1963).

7

IMPACT OF COMPUTER-BASED MANAGEMENT INFORMATION SYSTEMS ON ORGANIZATIONAL INFORMATION PROCESSING AND DECISION MAKING

COMMUNICATIONS WITHIN ORGANIZATIONS

The trend toward merging organizational communications with computerized networks is probably due to the demands for timely information, cost-effective data collection, and technologically advanced systems for processing information. The speed and preciseness with which a combined computer-communications system provides access to important information are paramount reasons for its increased use in diverse organizational environments (Churchill, Kempster, & Uretsky, 1969). MISs usually contain many types of communications that are permitted either explicitly or implicitly by management. From this broad perspective, MISs "include all activities in the regulative, innovative, integrative, and informative-instructive communication networks, whether the activities were external or internal, informal or formal, low programmed or high programmed, or whether interpersonal, small group or organization-wide" (Greenbaum, 1974, p. 745).

Computerized systems can, of course, initiate and produce changes in an organization's communications network. This is especially so in regard to the development and dispersion of nonvertical flow of information through the management structure. According to one author (Reif, 1968), this underscores the fact that MIS-induced communication changes have been limited primarily to informal information networks. At this point, hardly any changes have been made in formal organizational structures. Northrop (1965) questions Reif's assertion on the grounds that computerized information systems not only minimize transmission delays, but also optimize many managerial activities—sorting, searching, comparing, and correlating. These improved functional capabilities can also be incorporated into the formal, hierarchical, managerial communication system. If MISs are indeed integrated into these formal information networks, then their consequences must still be determined. Thus Lipstreu (1960) asks whether there will be an increase or decrease in the amount of direct, personal communication not only among managers, but also between managers and their underlings.

The implementation of MISs naturally alters the flow of information. Care should be taken to incorporate as part of the computerized communications system the former informal information network. Otherwise, a newly designed and developed MIS will be incomplete as far as the real flow of information in the organization is concerned (Mann & Williams, 1960). Since the introduction of MISs usually initiate noticeable changes in the channels of communications, many managers and employees become anxious and fearful, not knowing how these altered information flows may affect their situations. At times, some of these individuals react by attempting to do just about anything to resist the introduction and implementation of an innovative MIS that might modify their employment predicament (Hoos, 1960).

Another problem that is expected to accompany the implementation of an MIS is the "inversion of formerly normal superior-subordinate relationships" (Reynolds, 1969). It may be easier for a lower-level manager "to program" middle or top management if he has access to and control of an MIS terminal. The system can readily be programmed to display an absence of any real organizational problems and uncertainties and thus easily elicit from upper management the decision considered by the lower-level manager. This is the managerial equivalent of the "tail wagging the dog." Organizational entities such as chain-of-command, direct supervision, and mediated communication can easily be undermined by the utilization of an MIS, since face-to-face communication among people will likely decrease substantially and be replaced by interaction with a computerized information system (Whisler, 1965). Needless to say, it would be a gross error to restrict a significant amount of formal organizational communications exclusively to interactions with the automated information system. Not only will "the human element . . . [be] neglected in our computerized, systematized, mathematized world" (Conomikes, 1967), but a severe communications gap will likely exist within the organization. Another kind of information gap that could be created by MIS is a lack of communication between the automated systems people and the potential users (Slater, 1967). Finally, a communications gap could even occur among the different MISs being utilized within the same organization ("An overview of," 1969), especially if no earnest attempt is made to federate these formerly independent systems.

FLOW OF INFORMATION THROUGH ORGANIZATIONS

Only recently has information been identified and valued as an organizational resource having utility to management. Without the proper flow of information, it is impossible to run operations effectively and to plan an organization's future objectives in a rational way (Johnson & Derman, 1970). It is evident that "information flow in a communication network is the lifeline of a business enterprise; it is like blood flowing through the veins and arteries of the body" (Eilon, 1968). The primary means an executive has at his disposal to manage his other resources, human and material, is information. This resource is so vital to an enterprise that a considerable number of personnel and dollars are usually allocated to establish and maintain communication networks (Drucker, 1954). In a very real sense, management is tied to all of an organization's resources via its most fundamental resource—the information that flows through its communication channels. How readily information is transmitted among managers, and between managers and employees, is a sensitive standard by which to evaluate an organization's behavior. Since upper management levels are usually remote from organizational resources, the greater the number of intermediate managers, the more probable the delays and distortions in information flow. A computerized system can surmount these impediments by providing technology that speeds the dissemination of precise and appropriate information through an organizational hierarchy (Rowe, 1962).

According to Bedged-Dov (1967), the tremendous advantages derived from an MIS may be more easily evaluated if some of the defects of the traditional information systems are identified. With conventional communication networks, status reports frequently fail to arrive on time. If they do reach the proper manager, they often fail to include information commensurate with an executive's responsibilities. Further difficulties are encountered in carrying out planning functions due to the lack of relevant information, or the tedium involved in summarizing and formating reams of unprocessed data. At times, the information provided to a manager is so incomplete that it is impossible for him to take any rational action until additional details are defined. Also, there are instances when so many irrelevant reports are coming in to a manager that he is simply swamped. This generates excessive "noisy" input, so that executives sometimes find it extremely difficult to detect some of those critical situations and indices that have serious consequences for the organization.

The adoption and implementation of an MIS should make the formal information flow through an organization more concise and precise. Such a system might even force organizational members to use a more standardized language that ultimately facilitates communication. This could even be the case regarding interdepartmental communication, which is also improved by computerized information storage and retrieval systems ("How the computer," 1967). If MISs are to improve the information flow through an organization and also have real utility for management, the system should be designed in accordance with the following guidelines. The information contained in such a computerized system should be pertinent to managerial decision making. This implies that it should be presented precisely and quickly, and also as cost-effectively as possible. Also, the information displayed by the system should have a certain "actionability" about it, that is, it should be accessible to individuals of enough influence and power to effectuate organizational action (Hirsh, 1968).

Computerized information systems make it possible to produce reams of data that far exceeds the normal manager's information-processing capacity. Consequently, organizations sometimes train management teams to digest the horrendous quantities of complicated information output (Argyris, 1966a). In many large organizations, it is practically impossible to process such huge amounts of information without some highly systemized and computerized communications network (Daniel, 1961). However, there are times when some of these systems produce information that executives do not find appropriate to their problem-solving needs. A large amount of the information that is actually demanded by management concerns the organization's external environment; yet this is precisely the information that is usually not maintained within MISs. Such outside information is crucial for the adaptability and longevity of an organization, but it is often found lacking by top-level management. These individuals must respond even more to the extrinsic pressures on their organization than to intrinsic informational inputs.

It is usually lower-level management that responds to programmed output from MISs regarding indigenous organizational events. If higher management strata were to react to this truncated information, they would run the risk of "source distortion." These top executives must have access via their computerized systems to external, as well as internal, information (Keegan, 1974; Schoderbek & Schoderbek, 1971). Care should be taken, however, when attempting to identify and define the specifications for an MIS, not to press top-level managers too hard regarding their information requirements. It seems that these individuals find it very difficult to state clearly the precise characteristics of their informational demands, because of their global perspectives on external organizational environments (Daniel, 1961). Another difficulty that must be surmounted when implementing these systems is the consolidating, summarizing, or editing of information. Evidently, these editing techniques tend "to select data that are quantifiable, manageable, rational, and acceptable to management. . . . The computer [will be inclined] to accentuate the editorial coloration of organizational reporting systems in the direction of repressing vital information that does not fit the pipes in the channel" (Field, 1970, pp. 32-33).

One of the primary advantages of MIS is that computerized communication channels can be created that are contoured to the actual flow of information within the organization (Diebold, 1965). Not only might such a system decrease the uncertainty intrinsic to decision making, but it could certainly increase the number of action alternatives available. Obviously, if this is so, then any organization that implements automated information systems should have a tremendous competitive advantage with its ability to process information in an effective and efficient manner (Albaum, 1964). This assumes that firms that have this computerized capability do not underutilize these systems for problem-solving purposes (Vergin, 1967). Needless to say, the proper, formal flow of information through a firm is the wherewithal of optimal decision making (Cyert, Simon, & Trow, 1956). Some of this problem-solving skill may be ascribed to the processes of selecting or filtering information, which is usually exercised prior to its inclusion in an MIS. This should speed up the transmission of information through a firm, and thus minimize the delays in managerial decision making. Also, this expeditious dissemination of information may tend to establish more uniform objectives throughout an organization (Whisler & Shultz, 1960). Before the introduction of MISs, many firms found it troublesome to distribute, accurately and speedily, pertinent information to nodal decision makers ("How the computer," 1967). However, with the creation of computerized communication channels, this kind of transmission is highly probable. Because of it, the exact locus of decision-making power becomes highly visible. Some managers may experience an unexpectedly high level of anxiety due to the undisputed responsibility for decision making they incur by virtue of the information system's design.

It seems that middle management uses MISs more frequently to analyze certain situations than to identify specific problems. This tendency has several indirect implications for top management's decision making. According to Brady (1967), top-level executives are now more often able to

[a] Make some decisions at an earlier date.
[b] Gain time in which to consider some decisions.

[c] Review several courses of action before deciding what to do, rather than have but one recommended course to consider.
[d] Examine analyses of the impact that recommended courses of action will have on the problem or opportunity identified.
[e] Obtain additional detailed information from middle managers concerning problems, opportunities, and promising alternatives before making decisions. (p. 70)

As a result, more innovative thought regarding alternative solutions is being exercised by top management than middle management. Yet this does not preclude these intermediate managers from making decisions delegated to them by top-level managers. In fact, due to the installation of MISs, many middle and lower managers are making more decisions concerning an organization's operational requirements (Shaul, 1964). It appears that with the implementation of computerized information systems, at least some uncertainty is reduced and feedback loops established, so that more dynamic decision making becomes very likely (Ahlers, 1975). However, as managers find themselves interacting more and more with automated information systems, they may confer much less with their colleagues. Contrarily, these programmed systems may actually encourage personal interaction simply by increasing the time available for these activities (Gilman, 1966).

DECISION SYSTEMS USED BY ORGANIZATIONS

An organizational decision system usually consists of a mathematical model integrated with an MIS to assist managers in their problem-solving processes. These decision support systems emphasize the following: (a) a hierarchy among the many models that are linked together to serve as several solutions to distinct issues, (b) a framework for facilitating the interaction between the decision maker and other system components, (c) a structure that necessitates intricate interfaces and linkages among data banks, and (d) a cybernetic capability for dynamically updating and adapting decision paradigms. Decision systems of this sort are used not only in several operation areas, but also within separate managerial strata (Sprague & Watson, 1975a, 1975b). In order to implement these computerized decision aids, organizations should be considered as goal-seeking systems themselves. Also, to be additionally amenable to computerized decision systems, "the various activities, flows, responses, and behavioral characteristics" within an organization should be specified and analyzed in advance of automation. According to Gilman (1966), "successful use of the computer in decision making demands that we identify, classify, and weigh every decision and decision-situation that is significant to organizational performance. . . . This process of objective self-study brings about most of the organizational changes that are charged to the computer. The computer makes us look at our organization with close to complete objectivity, usually, for the first time. . . . [S]elf-analysis is bound to change the structure and the processes of the organization" (p. 79). With this done, the numerous decision nodes within the organization can be identified. Knitted together, they form the information and decision framework of the organization. Consequently, an organization can be considered an information- and decision-processing structure (Malcolm & Rowe, 1961; Rowe, 1962).

A manager within such a structure can be considered a nodal information processor and decision maker. The information flowing through these individuals can intermittently introduce time lags into the organizational network. The rate of information input, together with the time taken to make a decision, usually specify the queuing effect ascribed to a single manager (Rowe, 1961). A well-implemented MIS can easily improve the effectiveness of this information processing and decision making by minimizing the queuing effect. In turn, the flow of information and decisions through the total organization is definitely improved by reducing the time lags that critically impede system performance. Having a computerized information system will improve a manager's ability to make additional decisions by providing him with rapid feedback concerning the outcome of his choices (Ahlers, 1975). In order for this to occur, however, all the important information requirements for each nodal decision maker must be clearly defined (Taylor & Dean, 1966). A well-implemented MIS can surmount problems attributed to typical interaction patterns between transmitters and receivers of information within organizations. Some of these difficulties ascribed to interaction patterns are delineated by Albaum (1964) as follows:

1. Decision-makers frequently do not know what information is available because they do not know where to search for it or others in the organization fail to inform them of its availability. Perhaps even more fundamental, decision-makers often do not know what information they need—a

situation that can be ascribed to a large extent to a lack of experience in using various kinds of information.

2. Individuals who possess information do not pass it on to others in the company either for personal reasons or because they lack knowledge of who might need the information.
3. Distortion may occur as information is transmitted through an organization. (p. 31)

Another advantage attributed to an MIS is that organizational objectives can be explicitly stated and subjected to systematic analyses. That is, a greater number of decision alternatives can be evaluated, and a prolonged chain of cause-effect relationships studied. Consequently, the quality of organizational decision making should improve (Argyris, 1966a).

Not all events or outcomes attributed to the introduction and implementation of an MIS are completely profitable. It seems likely that the urge of subordinates to program managers in the same way that computers are programmed to make decisions will intensify due to MIS utilization. This may even occur to the extent that the relationship between executive status in the organization and the degree to which decisions are programmed is inverted (Reynolds, 1969). It may very well be that top managers will not make decisions at all. Their discretionary powers may be truncated, usurped, and dictated by those who design, develop, and maintain the MIS. It should be stressed, then, that the effect of MIS implementation on an organization's decision-making processes may be direct or indirect. This is especially true since "the <u>power</u> to make decisions and the <u>ability</u> to make decisions have become separated in the modern bureaucracy. This is frustrating both to the executive with the power and the specialist with the ability" (Reynolds, 1969). It appears that, more than ever, specified decision alternatives will be identified and defined by those lower down in the organizational hierarchy. A wise executive must be aware of the constraints imposed by the mediate or immediate consequences of MIS usage on his discretionary power.

DECISION STRUCTURE OF ORGANIZATIONS

Many individuals have indicated that an undoubted effect of MIS utilization is the centralization of the decision-making structure within the organization. These computerized systems certainly cause (1) a consolidation and integration of decentralized decision systems, (2) a movement of decision-making responsibility toward the top of the managerial hierarchy, (3) a rationalization and quantification of discretionary activity, (4) a crucial change in decision making at the middle management level, and (5) a beginning of rigidity and inflexibility in decision-making processes. Also, with the continuing creation of larger capacity MISs, it is highly likely that a smaller number of executives will exercise discretionary responsibility (Whisler, 1970a). It seems that the authority for making structured, as well as unstructured, decisions will be allocated to nodal positions within the organization. It is at these points that computerized information will be disseminated to facilitate managerial decision making (Anshen, 1960).

Some of the factors that account for this trend toward centralization are additional standardization, increased control, operational consolidation, and instant feedback, all of which can be ascribed to MIS usage. Because of these attributes, lower-level management is making fewer important decisions, and higher-level management is exercising greater operational control. Along with this trend toward more centralization of decision making, has come the increased concern of organizations to be extremely discriminating in designating exactly who will make the decisions (Reif, 1968). At times, the organization's problem-solving environment takes on the appearance of a "war room" (Krauss, 1970), especially if the massive data bases required to support MIS systems are available. New computerized systems make available techniques that can easily handle the organization's complex information requirements. This technology is a further force for centralizing the decision structure (Whisler & Shultz, 1960). Also, the difficulties attributed to the "cascading effect of decisions" due to differing problem definitions and performance measures that exist at distinct organizational levels can be surmounted by MIS usage (Rowe, 1961).

Yet several individuals indicate, on the contrary, that MISs have a decentralizing effect on the decision-making structure. Just as computerized systems can bring information to centrally located managers to improve their decision making, these systems can bring information to peripherally located managers to improve their decision making too (Jones, 1970). There are times when such a decentralized decision network can be more advantageous than a centralized network. This is especially so when outlying operating personnel, because of their location, need more immediate information than internal managing personnel. Modern information technology readily provides the capability for creating such decentralized decision-making structures. One consequence of this could be that peripheral personnel will have more discretionary responsibility, since they will now have access to information needed for decision making (Drucker, 1966). Because information is provided quickly and accurately by computerized communication networks, decision making can be delegated further down the organization structure (Moan, 1973). These systems may also liberate many lower-level managers from much tedium and permit them to partake of additional decision-making duties. Yet, on the other hand, MIS implementation may necessarily preclude the delegation of discretionary activities down the organizational hierarchy. There could be, instead, an increased tendency to centralize the decision-making network. According to Dale's (1964) survey, neither trend has dominated the decision-making environment.

It is interesting to note that Mulder (1960) defines decision structure in terms of "who makes decisions for whom." Groups with a more centralized network should be capable of improved judgmental performance, since recommendations from members can be processed and consolidated by a centrally located decision maker. Yet such a centralized structure has a certain degree of "vulnerability" about it. That is, since most of the group's interaction is through this nodal position, any commotion here will be quickly radiated outward to peripheral members. With the central position inoperative, it would be impossible for information to flow among the other members of the group. Shaw (1954a; 1954b), however, states that "availability of information" to all members of a decision-making group, is important not only for simple problems, but for complex problems as well. This is especially so regarding the speed with which complex tasks are completed by decentralized networks. Obviously, this is contrary to Mulder's notion that increased centralization of the decision structure improves group performance. Mulder stresses the necessity for integrating members' information-processing contributions independently of task complexity. Shaw theorizes that within centralized networks the person occupying the nodal position could easily become "saturated" with input information. That is, he would likely suffer from information overload. Mulder demonstrates, however, that this is not the case. The centralized decision maker does not experience a greater information flow into, or out of, his position. A centralized group, though, is more vulnerable than a decentralized group.

In regard to this issue, Becker and Baloff (1969) claim that

> It may be meaningless to characterize a group as 'tightly or loosely' organized, or as 'centralized or decentralized' . . . a group can be tight or centralized with regard to one or two of the three components and loose or decentralized with regard to another. For example, a group can be organized tightly for information processing, loosely for decision making, and either

> tightly or loosely for generating alternatives from all members. In such cases the dichotomous designations, 'tight-loose' and 'centralized-decentralized' would not be useful. (p. 268)

They indicate that in most investigations of micro communication channels, centralization is determined by physical location within the network. However, in formal macro organizations, the structure of decision-making positions is hierarchical. Consequently, it is doubtful that findings from small-group experimental studies can be extrapolated to large organizational entities. Also, "the contradictions in the literature exist because researchers manipulate positions in a communication system and make conclusions about centralization, and assign information-exchange tasks and draw conclusions about problem-solving behavior" (Becker & Baloff, 1966, p. 261).

According to Argyris (1966b), "the more management deals with complexity by the use of computers and quantitative approaches, the more it will be forced to work with inputs of many different people, and the more important will be the group dynamics of decision-making meetings" (p. 95). Contrary to common belief, groups may not have a conservative influence on their members. Ziller (1957) establishes that more risky decisions are made in situations where the entire group has discretionary power than in situations where such power is restricted to the leader of the group. Marquis (1962) demonstrates that after group discussion, members tend to alter their decision-making behavior in the direction of greater risk taking. This change is characteristic not only of unanimous group decisions, but also of individual decisions arrived at independently. Marquis also finds that this increased tendency to accept risk can not be ascribed to the spread of responsibility among group members. Finally, he points out that the dynamics animating this behavior are unknown.

Wallach and Kogan (1965) establish that group discussion results in a similar shift toward risk taking, whether or not consensus is reached. However, Wallach, Kogan, and Bem (1962) find that a change toward more riskiness occurs if decisions are made unanimously by a group; individual decisions made prior to discussion tend to be less risky. However, if individual decisions are made following group discussion, this same alteration toward more riskiness occurs. They suggest that spreading of responsibility among group members may account for this risky shift. Marquis claims that it can be ascribed to an enhancement of role expectations because of group interaction, or to an increased influence by individuals who are more inclined to take risks. Shaw (1971) suggests that it is due to (a) the utility of risk for some roles; (b) the cultural value of risk taking; (c) the fact that individuals who are most inclined to take risks are also the most influential members within the group; and/or (d) the diffusion of responsibility in group behavior. But whatever the reason, the data are incontrovertible. If, in fact, as Argyris asserts, computerized systems encourage group decision making, then these systems will likely lead to greater risk taking. It remains to be seen, however, whether or not the timeliness and preciseness of the information provided by MISs, together with this shift toward more riskiness, will produce better decisions.

8
DESIGN OF COMPUTER-BASED MANAGEMENT INFORMATION SYSTEMS

NATURE OF INTEGRATED INFORMATION SYSTEMS

Initially, computers were used primarily for clerical tasks. Later on, they were employed as integral components of integrated information systems, storing, retrieving, and manipulating data in order to combine the communications requirements of the organization into an integrated information network. Typically, these computerized communication channels are constructed primarily to aid decision making (Anshen, 1969). The total organization is considered a complete communication system, whose information flows are funnelled through nodal decision makers responsible for improving the organization's performance (Koontz, 1959). Separate components of integrated MISs are usually designed within the context of the entire network, since it is realized in advance that the components impact on each other. The demand to combine these components into a unified network is seldom overlooked. Following the introduction of an integrated MIS, communication networks are often completely reconfigured to facilitate the flow of information (Vergin & Grimes, 1964). In order to integrate an MIS, it is absolutely necessary to federate the many different and independent data bases that exist in the organization, and it is essential to combine properly the many computerized paradigms, which process input information for these integrated systems (Schoderbek & Schoderbek, 1971). There also seems to be a relationship between the complexity of input to the complexity of output. "The more a system is differentiated and integrated . . . the more the potential information in the input is utilized in outputs" (Driver & Streufert, 1969). Consequently, it would be wise to plan an integrated MIS not only to combine the numerous decision nodes in an information network, but also to include the information requirements of many different organizational levels (Evans & Hague, 1962; Johnson, Fremont, & Rosenzweig, 1963). For the purpose of implementing an integrated MIS, an organization should be considered a cybernetic system that utilizes feedback, provided by the computerized communication's network, to reach its objectives. If a system is truly integrated, it should supply historical, on-line, real-time data for management (Crowley, 1966). Redundancies in the data and within the computer programs themselves should be eliminated (Horton, 1974). It is obvious that designing, developing, and driving an aggregation of distinct, independent, and automated information systems is not a very useful way to utilize computer technology (Dearden, 1965).

Yet several authors are, on the contrary, very skeptical about the success of integrated MISs. According to Poindexter (1969), "It's going to be easier to send a man to the moon than put together an integrated management information system." Dearden (1966) declares that these MISs do not necessarily depend on the utilization of real-time systems for providing instantaneous access to information. Moreover, to attempt to achieve integration via real-time systems is not only excruciatingly expensive, but also tremendously ineffective. Similarly, Schoderbek and Schoderbek (1971) state that even if it were possible to develop and implement integrated MISs, the data bases would have to be enormous. They also assert that "the quest for a total integrated system is sheer folly as well as misleading. The quantum jump from modular subsystems to one 'holistic' system is neither financially nor technically feasible at this time." Herschman (1968) points out that the incompatibility of many of the components adds to the difficulty of establishing an integrated system: they remain "islands of automation that can't be connected until we get commonality." Dearden (1972) says it is erroneous to believe that some sort of centralized control can be created over an organization's integrated information. It is also wrong to suppose that without this coordination the different communication networks would not be regularized in a satisfactory manner. He claims that "a company . . . [which] . . . pursues an MIS embarks on a wild-goose chase, a search for a will-o'-the-wisp."

DESIGN PRINCIPLES FOR COMPUTER-BASED MANAGEMENT INFORMATION SYSTEMS

In light of the enormous expense of computerized systems, it is astonishing how skimpy the research is concerning the problem of MIS design (Stern, 1971). Even without a sufficient knowledge base, "major companies have mounted massive efforts aimed at designing MIS[s] with results ranging from disaster to partial success. It is still appropriate to say that well-designed and operating MIS[s] are much easier to find in the pages of technical and management journals than in real life" (Fredericks, 1971, p. 7). It seems that no methodical or universal theory exists that is adequate for the proper planning of MISs. However, some specific standards have surfaced and should form the basis of MIS design: (1) an MIS is not a superficial system to be applied to an already functional organizational structure; (2) an MIS must be intrinsically incorporated into a firm's information system; (3) an MIS should be considered the technological subsystem of an organization viewed as a man-machine system (Simon, 1967).

It should be emphasized that within such a sociotechnical system, tasks are distributed between man and machine components according to their respective capacities and costs (Simon, 1967). The crucial factor in designing these systems is specifying the nature of the symbiotic relationship between the human and computer components. What needs to be established is "the point at which the computer should replace man, the point at which it should assist him . . ., and the point at which it should not be used. At present, these unresolved issues are still met by automating any function which can be described precisely enough to program and by letting man improvise on those functions which cannot be programmed. More definitive design principles for these key issues must be forthcoming" (Mayer, 1970, p. 179). Similarly, it is critical when planning those sociotechnical systems that man's role be designed so that his job is intrinsically motivating (Jordan, 1962). Otherwise, behavioral problems linked to the design and development of MISs may arise. If these design snares are detected beforehand, then the chances of creating a successful system increase.

Designing an MIS exclusively according to management principles guarantees neither superior problem solving, nor improved decision making. It would be a gross error to plan an MIS without complete concern for the human factor. After all is said and done, this is the dimension that ultimately determines whether or not an MIS will be successful. It is extremely important that the designer of an MIS be cognizant of the following statement by Neel (1971):

> An information system, as it really exists, is part of the social system of the organization. Participation, if done willingly, usually indicates that the system has become part of the social environment of the organization. Although this information system design may not look as good on paper, or not be an optimum system,

> its acceptance as part of the social character of the organization will almost always assure its workability. (p. 38)

Also, according to Neel, an MIS can be created in such a way that it becomes the basis for an organizational incentive system: individuals will be aware that their performance is to be evaluated in terms of their information inputs to the MIS. Finally, it is of paramount importance that these computerized systems be planned so that the broad distribution of individual differences that exist within an organization are taken into account. In this way, the performances of many different individuals can be optimized within the "computer-aided environment." What Sackman (1970) calls "social effectiveness" is thus designed into the MIS.

A number of personnel, each of whom possesses a specific expertise, must be involved in the design and development of MISs, because of the complexity, differentiation, and federation of the many components of an integrated information system. It is highly unlikely that a single individual could possess, in sufficient depth, all the knowledge required to plan an effective MIS. "The selection, aggregation, and manipulation of data are matters where knowledge, not mere know-how, must be applied" (Hoos, 1971). Also, there are instances when managers themselves attempt to hoard as much information as possible. Apparently, this is done to increase their perceived prestige and/or the permanency of their positions. Not only does this result in the redundancy of information, but also it places a needless demand on the output of the MIS. To surmount these irksome impediments, the design of computerized communication systems should be decision oriented. That is, information should be made available to a manager primarily for problem solving (Neel, 1971). Carefully chosen information should be incorporated into the MIS to assist the manager in his judgments regarding organizational planning, controlling, and evaluating (Holmes, 1970). However, this does not necessitate designing an MIS for specific functional areas such as finance and operations. If this were done, it would be difficult to give proper consideration to the interrelated information requirements that exist among dependent activities (Porter & Mulvihill, 1965). Those who plan an MIS should be constantly aware of the objectives of individual departments, and also capable of reducing judgments to computerized algorithms (Malcolm & Rowe, 1961). It is important to plan an MIS so that it is compatible to the particularities of specific operating systems. "If an operating system is loose then there is an obvious need for real-time human management, and therefore an obvious need for collecting information that will enable managers to make interim choices. If, on the other hand, the operating system is tight there is less need for real-time human management, and therefore much less need for an information flow which has as its aim, the strengthening of decisions about current operations" (Beckett, 1965, p. 67).

It seems improbable that an effective MIS could be created by following the flow of a firm's existing information network. Design specifications for MISs should be selected so that they are independent of those used to plan the previously employed information system. Basing the plans for an MIS on current policy manuals, job descriptions, and organizational charts will not likely lead to a satisfactory system. These materials were developed within the context of the existing organizational structure. As such, it is highly improbable that a totally new computerized communication system can be created, which is independent of an organization's static structure. Theoretically, it is much better to plan an MIS apart from the firm's existing information system. In order to design an ideal MIS, it is necessary to specify in advance crucial decision nodes in the network. Thus, information can be channelled so that it reaches the proper people for discretionary purposes.

There seem to be a few primary determinants involved in MIS design. These include available technology and data bases, proposed organizational strategy and structure, and managerial and judgmental mechanics (Zani, 1970). Some principles for MIS planning can be specified. Wilkinson (1974, pp. 36-37) proposes that MIS does the following:

1. Provides relevant information to managers and other users.
2. Operates in an efficient and economical manner.
3. Insures accurate and accessible information.
4. Provides information with appropriate timeliness.
5. Operates with an integrated and consistent framework.
6. Exhibits simplicity of operation.
7. Provides adequate capacity for all legitimate needs.
8. Maintains sufficient flexibility, versatility, adaptability, and stability with respect to changing needs and conditions.
9. Motivates managers and employees to act in ways that promote the organization's objectives.

Beged-Dov (1967, p. B-826) supplements these guidelines: a well-planned MIS should, in addition,

(1) Provide each level and position of management with all the information that can be used in the conduct of each manager's job.
(2) Filter the information so that each level and position of management actually receives only the information it can and must act on.
(3) Provide information to the manager only when action is possible and appropriate.
(4) Provide information that is up to date in a form that is easily understood and digested by the manager.

Finally, an MIS should be designed to yield not only pure information, but also informative feedback, so that the organization can better adapt itself to specific situations (Porter & Mulvihill, 1965). With this additional capability, the firm's behavior more closely approximates that of a true cybernetic system. A closed-looped feedback system is more effective than an open-loop information system in helping an organization to achieve its goals.

The above principles for the design of MISs are representative of the guidelines that appear in the literature. What are lacking are empirically derived data assessing the several system design strategies. Some data obtained during semi-structured interviews of managers, scientists, and engineers indicate that the following steps should be used for the design of MISs:

1. The <u>need</u> for the system should be made explicit;
2. The decision-making <u>objectives</u> of the system should be established;
3. The <u>personnel</u> impacted by the system should be identified;
4. The <u>outputs</u> of the system should be defined;
5. The <u>problems and overlapping areas</u> in the system should be determined;
6. The need for <u>flexibility</u> within the system should be specified;
7. The methods of <u>data collection</u> should be delineated;
8. The planned design <u>procedures</u> should be specified;
9. The <u>mechanisms</u> for obtaining system feedback should be generated (Holland, Kretlow, & Ligon, 1974, p. 14).

These guidelines for system design seem consonant with those principles already mentioned and with those steps mentioned elsewhere in the literature (Ackoff, 1967; Seese, 1970). It appears then that there is at least some agreement between the theoreticians and practitioners regarding MIS design.

A major obstacle that must be overcome in order to plan and implement an MIS is the absence not only of fast and suitable systems for data-based management systems, but also of sufficiently vast data files. The essential issue of MIS design is the consolidation of tremendous amounts of data for effective utilization by management (Ein-Dor, 1975). Compatability among the computer files is essential for a functional system ("The corporate data," 1966). It is very important that MISs be configured to enable individuals to access on demand various data files. Having this capability should permit personnel to relate readily the contents of one file with another ("The corporate data," 1966).

There are several technical developments that should facilitate the design of improved MISs:

> 1. The current state of data communications is probably the major obstacle to overcome in the near future if real-time and time-sharing applications are to reach their potential. . . .
> 2. The man-machine interface will be significantly improved as direct interrogation of the computer is made through improved keyboard or voice input. . . . The real task in developing these systems is managerial, not hardware. The design and structuring of the system will be aided as managers participate in design in a more meaningful way. . . .
> 3. Large data bases will become more common as the cost of storage continues to decrease. Cost reductions and the expanded use of random access files and memory will permit the substitution of an integrated data base for the multiplicity of independent files now maintained.
> 4. Present input/output devices have been the bottleneck to full use of the computer processor (Murdick & Ross, 1972, p. 32).

Also, advances in computer science and communications technology suggest that within this decade MISs will have at least a few of the following capabilities:

> 1. High capacity random access storage will permit the formation of a central data file containing the entire data input which may be needed in the company for a wide range of purposes, including of

course the operation of a management information system. That is, a common data base will replace the numerous existing files. Data format will be standardized which will permit the use of a single data base in a large number of applications.

2. Reduced communication data collection and data processing costs will encourage the use of "real time" systems capable of reflecting events as they occur. Time sharing will become increasingly common.
3. Systems flexibility for new applications will be increased, and the costs to the user reduced through a broad range of new peripheral equipment developments. These advances will be in two areas; in the improved performance of special purpose equipment such as data collection stations, and in the development of relatively inexpensive remote inquiry and display devices.
4. A totally new data storage and processing capability—(graphic storage and processing)—will become economical and commonly available.
5. Information retrieval will become an increasingly important aspect of information systems. Direct system interrogation, at a desired level of detail, will take place through remote inquiry devices, and response from the computers will be in the form of printed, displayed, or audio media.
6. Small desk size computers having the power of some medium size computers of today will be made available to individual managers, engineers, designers, and even clerks.
7. Telephone sets will tie our homes to a central computing facility. Basic arithmetic computations will be executed by pressing the appropriate buttons on the set. The computer will reply in a voice mode. (Beged-Dov, 1967, pp. B-828-B-829)

In order to design a useful MIS, a system planner's perspective should incorporate the views of the managers who will use it—that is, looking down from the top of the organizational pyramid. It seems that the proper planning of these systems begins with management itself. Executives are cognizant of, and responsible for, a firm's objectives, structures, decisions, strategies, and tactics. These elements must be specified and consolidated into the design of the MIS (Zani, 1970). Obviously, management should also be aware of the internal and external environments in which the organization operates. This knowledge should be used too as a resource for further refining the requirements of the MIS (Elliott, 1974). Likewise, the experience and expertise of operating managers should be utilized in MIS design to assure its compatibility with functional needs (Clayton, 1973). A planning procedure that emphasizes adherence to a management-oriented system should prevail throughout the entire design phase (Hanold, 1968). The basis for constructing this sort of system is establishment of each executive's information requirements (Daniel, 1961). If this is not done, then at least a few firms will more than likely devalue the utility of MISs universally (Zani, 1970).

Designing usable systems demands not only the awareness of management's information needs, but also the knowledge of many different disciplines. The range of expertise required to design and develop these systems extends from management and computer sciences to psychological and social sciences ("Data management," 1970). Regardless of what pool of knowledge is chosen as a working context, it is absolutely essential for the success of an MIS that the user's criteria of system acceptability be specified as precisely as possible (Peace & Easterby, 1973). This should be done prior to actual planning, or at least no later than the early design stages. In many cases, managers are asked not only about their information necessities, but also about their specifications for sufficient system performance. The implication here is that management can identify and define these requirements. However, there is some evidence that suggests that this is not true, and that management will be unable to translate the policies by which decisions are made (Beged-Dov, 1967; Schoderbek & Schoderbek, 1971). Obviously, this will limit the designer's ability to create an MIS that supports the decision maker. Even if an executive has excellent judgmental abilities, there is no reason to expect these skills to transfer spontaneously into the design and function of an MIS (Simon, 1960c). Somehow a manager's discretionary capabilities or processes must be objectified, in order to be incorporated into the planning and working of a computerized system.

In order to implement an MIS, it is also necessary to create a centrally controlled cluster of data definitions and formats. This will produce a homogeneous grouping of data files within the organization, which can readily serve many different "public" users. Having consistent data should minimize problems associated with retrieval and analysis of files with dissimilar data definitions and formats. Needless to say, designing such a set of files is not an easy undertaking, since it requires nothing less than centralized control and optimal organization. However, this commonality among formats and data definitions does not demand a centrally located facility for these files. What is needed is the assurance that each user will not develop his own data definitions ("The corporate data," 1966). Thus, the data base must be structured in a way that enables a large number of syncretic requirements to employ this organizational memory (Wilkinson, 1974).

There are instances when decision algorithms, which have been developed as intrinsic aspects of an MIS, have fallen into disuse because sufficient data bases have not been established. For each run of these models, additional data must be collected, and this can become very costly. Also, many algorithms for decision making have not been consolidated into an MIS. Instead of incorporating these paradigms into an integrated system, they are usually used singly and independently. These models should be developed so as to be compatible with one another and to form a consolidated system. Also, they should be designed to receive most of their inputs from a centrally controlled data base, and to store most of their outputs here as well. This output can then be used as input on some subsequent occasion (Sprague & Watson, 1975a).

An analysis of the sort of managerial decisions being made in the organization is a definite prerequisite for good MIS design. Usually, decisions exercised by management can be classified as follows:

(a) Decisions for which adequate models are available or can be constructed and from which optimal (or near optimal) solutions can be derived. In such cases the decision process itself should be incorporated into the information system thereby converting it (at least partially) to a control system. A decision model identifies what information is required and hence what information is relevant.

(b) Decisions for which adequate models can be constructed but from which optimal solutions cannot be extracted. Here some kind of heuristic or search procedure should be provided even if it consists of no more than computerized trial and error. A simulation of the model will, as a minimum, permit comparison of proposed alternative solutions. Here too the model specifies what information is required.

(c) Decisions for which adequate models cannot be constructed. Research is required here to determine what information is relevant. If decision making cannot be delayed for the completion of

> such research or the decision's effect is not large enough to justify the cost of research, then judgment must be used to "guess" what information is relevant. It may be possible to make explicit the implicit model used by the decision maker and treat it as a model of type (b). (Ackoff, 1967, p. 184)

Obviously, complete analysis of the types of judgments made by management should yield information regarding the design of the MIS, as well as the areas where the computer can assist the decision maker. This analysis may also produce some insights into how the information should be structured, and its optimal arrival rate (Rowe, 1962). Decision analysis is especially critical to the design of MISs in military environments, since, in these situations, MISs are particularized by many attributes not normally associated with civilian systems, specifically, secrecy, speed, and exceedingly high reliability (Mayer, 1970). Attempting to configure appropriate systems for these military environments is a very difficult task that demands the federation of many different data bases.

There has been much debate between managerial and systems personnel concerning the specifications of ideal designs for MISs. Many of these systems experts believe that they know what the ultimate MIS should be: "They conjure up visions of the company chief executive sitting in his oak-paneled office asking the most complex and esoteric questions of his own private crystal ball: the cathode-ray-tube console" (Herschman, 1968). At times these MIS experts are rather intimidating to management, who perceive them as attempting to impose their own technological biases upon systems-nescient executives. Consequently, these systems men are usually criticized as technocrats, dehumanized men who are insensitive toward people, and who manipulate situations in order to impose their objectives on others (Balk, 1971). MIS designers should be more sensitive toward the feelings of management and more aware of the "politics" involved in organizational behavior. In the long run, it may be beneficial for these specialists to give in sometimes to the demands of systems-ignorant management, if this can be done without sacrificing MIS integrity. This is especially so if MISs are planned "so that they adapt to the psychological constellation which each of the individual users brings to the task situation" (Wynne & Dickson, 1975). If a system is designed so that it does not meet management's specific requirements, "then clearly the so-called 'management information system' is merely a mechanism for cluttering managers' desks with costly, voluminous, and probably irrelevant printouts" (Zani, 1970).

9
CONCLUSIONS AND RECOMMENDATIONS

MANAGERIAL PERFORMANCE AND DECISION MAKING

In summary, many of the problems that arise from the implementation of MISs upon managerial performance and decision making have been fully identified and comprehensively discussed. It appears that the scope and complexity of management itself will increase because of the impact of MISs. These systems could also modify the dimensions traditionally attributed to the practice of management by eliminating challenge, responsibility, opportunity, and reward. Even the ease with which managers are recruited may change because of MIS implementation. Some individuals, however, foresee little change. They believe that these systems will not usurp the duties of management, but only routinize internal practices, or assist managerial decision making.

The introduction and utilization of MISs will not have the same implications for top, middle, and lower management. It is projected that the greatest impact will occur in the top and middle management strata. The job content and managerial-skill requirements of top-level managers may change. The power and control vested in top management may also be in jeopardy due to MIS utilization and the possibility of programming in these high-level jobs, too. Other writers do not see the usurping of power and control from top managers, or the programming of their jobs. On the contrary, they assert that MISs will aid top managers by assisting them to view the organization as an "integrated system," and by facilitating their understanding of the total organization. It is the middle managers who will be most affected by the increased reliance on the computer.

Because of the utilization of MISs, decentralization of middle management's power and control will probably take place. Also, automating or programming middle management's typical tasks will likely eliminate all power and control these individuals may have had. Middle management will probably become very depersonalized, highly programmed, and more machine-like; consequently, middle-level managers will probably seek personal satisfaction off the job. The specific impact of MIS on middle management has not yet been settled. Very little research has been done to substantiate and identify exactly what has changed. Lower managers may be caught between the computerized production process and the MIS, each of which creates its own unique communications problem.

Regarding the impact of MIS implementation on the number of middle managers, the evidence is inconclusive. Early authors thought that middle managers would definitely be reduced in number by MISs, because of computerization of most of their tasks. Computerization was also expected to decrease managerial decision making, and thus, eventually, the ranks of middle management. Some writers disagreed: a few affirmed that the trend toward decentralization would continue in spite of the introduction of MISs, and that these systems would not decrease the numbers of middle managers. Although much monotonous administrative work would be eliminated because of MISs, there would be no accompanying reduction in middle manager ranks. These contradictions concerning the impact of computerized systems upon the number of middle managers underscore the need for further investigation.

There is another hindrance that must be considered prior to, during, and after MIS implementation: management's lack of technical knowledge concerning the system. As a result of this deficiency managers may feel threatened by technically skilled subordinates. Many writers have stressed the necessity for managerial participation and involvement in all phases—planning, developing, implementing, utilizing, and maintaining—of MIS. Without management involvement and participation, designers may produce systems that fail to meet managerial requirements. If management does not get involved, then how will designers of MISs know what information is needed for decision making? Managerial attitudes must be conducive to and supportive of the MIS. A "climate of rationality" must exist within the organizational environment. Managers should be MIS users: they should not remain aloof from the system, but should attempt, instead, to close the "communications gap" between themselves and the systems people.

Overwhelming inadequacies seem to exist in the education, knowledge, and skills of the manager/user. Management needs re-education in the new MISs; they must acquire whatever skills are necessary to work with the new information technology. They must educate themselves regarding the computer's contribution to decision making, and the stimulation of systems thinking. Otherwise, top management may be overwhelmed or bewildered by the young specialists trained in computer methods, and may lose contact with changes occurring in lower levels of management. Upper management should be computer literate if they want to survive, because MISs may initiate changes in management roles and challenge many long-established practices and doctrines. Some perceived threats due to MIS-initiated changes in management's environment include the following: replacement of managers; loss of security and status; encroachment on decision-making rights; increased usage of quantitative procedures; lack of basic understanding of the system; and incompetence exposed by the system.

As far as the general functions of management are concerned, MISs will alter not only the activities and tasks management is responsible for, but also the manager's "personal methods of operation." MISs will likely lead to changes in management's scope and perspective, as well as attitudes and philosophy, since management activities will no longer be tied to organizational status or position. The systemic approach to managerial jobs is a direct result of the introduction and utilization of an MIS. The traditional job characteristics of management—"goal setting, pattern perception, communication, and computation"—will be usurped or altered significantly by MIS. Some writers claim that MIS will have little impact on routine management activities; others claim that there will be some impact, and that management will serve the system. Again, some authors believe that management will spend proportionately more time on planning functions; others believe the opposite. The introduction of an MIS would probably not alter the amount of energy spent by management in the supervision of subordinates and in the coordination function. However, some writers think that supervising per se will be disrupted by MISs, resulting in lessening of job status and depersonalizing of individual relationships. Regarding the impact of MIS on the amount of time spent in the controlling function, there is again a diversity of findings and opinions. Management will probably spend more and more time on staffing activities; and there is bound to be a change in requirements of the positions to be filled. In short, the literature is full of contradictions concerning the impact of MIS on the traditional functions of management.

Concerning the roles of top management, some writers expect the following changes: (1) more focusing on change problems, (2) less involvement in routine decision making, (3) more use of simulation techniques in less structured judgment, and (4) more managers becoming technically obsolete sooner. The coordinating function of top management will become more time constrained. That is, MIS will be reducing time scales, thus creating more intense and diversified pressures on top management. Some authors also suggest that MISs will tend to centralize the management structure and facilitate decision making by circumventing lower management. The jobs of middle management may also be changed by MIS implementation, becoming highly structured and programmed. There would thus be a salient reduction in organizational status. Other writers, however, argue that MISs will expand the scope of middle management's job, making it much more complex than presently. Consequently, middle management's job status will more than likely increase because of information technology. Ambiguity does exist among the allegations concerning the changing content of middle management's job status. Are middle management jobs becoming more rewarding and demanding, or more punishing and lax, because of MIS utilization? The more pessimistic authors believe that these jobs will become less challenging, more routine, highly structured, exceedingly repetitive, and further formalized. Also, because of MIS implementation, middle management will probably relinquish its planning function. These executives will likely spend less time in controlling activities. The most severe impact of MIS will likely be upon the motivating and coordinating functions of middle management. This is a direct result of a substantial reduction in the number of subordinates, due to computerization of their tasks. More likely than not, middle management will spend more time attempting to motivate their subordinates.

A few writers claim that MISs will have no effect on the job of management. The MIS-produced "management revolution" will not occur, and management will retain power and control. These authors assert that MISs have not affected managers as predicted: promises have gone unfulfilled. Once implemented, MISs do not seem to be performing the functions designed into them. According to a few writers, middle managers have not been reduced in numbers, nor have their tasks become programmed. This is due probably to the tremendous variability of management's operational-type problems, plans, and decisions. Their tasks are too broad to be computerized. The projected demise of middle management status has not become a reality; and even top management has not been influenced as drastically as predicted: in fact, it has neither benefited nor changed. It seems that most MIS-produced output is processed by mid-level managers. This lack of effect on top management could be due to under-utilization of the MIS, "managerial inertia," very high expectations, shortage of qualified users, or lack of involvement.

One way to maximize the use of the manager's time is to design and develop an MDS to support him. In order to accomplish this task, it is important, first, to analyze what critical decisions have to be made; second, to establish effective strategies for making them; and third, to design a system that merges the decision maker, the mathematical models, the data bases, and the computational power of the mainframe. There is a trend toward automating more operational decisions, which will tend to alter managerial responsibilities by concentrating them more on developing automated decision rules and policies and by attempting to better the decision process. With the increased trend toward MDS implementation, managerial decision making is not only becoming more analytical and scientific, but is also relying less upon intuition and guesswork. However, it is very unlikely that MDSs can be programmed to mimic many of the complex decisions required by management. This is so since there are numerous intangibles and unspecifiable relationships that must be analyzed appropriately and objectively. Many parameters and variables inherent in managerial problems cannot be quantified. Consequently, some managers complain incessantly that "computer solutions" are completely inadequate for their specific decision-making situations. These programmed algorithms are apparently based on too many limiting assumptions and constraining conditions.

In programmed decision making, "decision discretion" is an essential aspect of the automated system itself. Here, the human component is no longer in the loop once the system is developed, so the decisions themselves are made without human judgment. A few authors firmly hold that many of the forecasts that proclaimed the programming of structured, as well as unstructured, decisions are not being realized very rapidly. Much of the difficulty encountered in programming these judgments is due primarily to the unstructured, inexact, and impending nature of the data demanded by managerial decisions. Not only are some managerial problems unstructured or unknown, but they are also continuously changing. Apparently, these programmed systems are just too rigid; they lack the flexibility of the human decision maker to consider new variables and relationships. It appears that an irreducible number of irregular and critical decisions will still have to be made by management.

Regarding the relationship of middle management to automated decision making, a few writers claim that organizations will be highly automated man-machine systems, where management itself will be modified by the system being managed. It seems that the computer has abrogated at least a few routine decisions that were typically exercised by middle management. Thus, many middle managers are extremely vulnerable to displacement. This might ultimately lead to a much smaller number of such executives in existing enterprises. Also, the managerial mystique often attributed to "judgment," "experience," and "creativity" cannot possibly withstand the inevitable intrusion of factual data bases, analytical algorithms, and automated decision systems. These MDSs, because of their explicit presumptions and judgmental policies, give managerial decision making an uncomfortable "visibility."

There are several consequences of MDSs for the decision maker. Current information supplied by an MDS permits management to make better informed, more itemized, and more rapid decisions. However, such a system may make the decision maker more "risky" because of diffusion of responsibility. If the outcome is not as it should be, then the manager can readily blame the computerized system itself, or its designer. Another implication of MDS is that decisions formerly made judgmentally by management can now be executed automatically by the computer. One salient result of this mechanization is the "de-personalization" of the discretionary process. The manager now passively receives alphanumeric or graphic cues that elicit his judgmental response. He is now manipulated by the computer—he has "a machine for a boss." Also, much of management's mistrust of automating decision making has to do with the inability of these systems to capture and incorporate "executive sensitivity or gut feel"—the nonquantifiable data that are important parts of managerial discretion.

With reference to the computerized decision system and information overload, some individuals caution against the "semantic pollution in information systems," which can undermine the effectiveness of MIS. The emphasis in designing MISs should be placed on purging irrelevant information; otherwise, undue attention will probably be dedicated to the "generation, storage, and retrieval" of information that is unrefined and unnecessary. The manner in which an MIS is employed must contribute to the solution of managerial problems. An MIS can accomplish this if it is configured to the prevailing decision environment to which it inputs information. At least one salient reason for installing an MIS is to surmount the limited information upon which most decisions are based. To accomplish this, it is necessary to insure that the desired information can be easily and efficiently elicited from the system upon demand. It should be stressed that inadequate information systems "cannot be corrected by a computer." According to some authors, the attempt to automate information systems is the incorrect procedure for solving problems that arise from lack of information.

It appears to some authors that information load is driven to the point of information "overload" or "glut" by the capacity of computers to accumulate and generate reams of information. Most MISs are designed and developed on the assumption that most managers operate with a "lack of relevant information." However, it seems that with MIS managers experience a superabundance of irrelevant information. Benefits derived from MISs are contingent on the proper input to the computerized system. When unpurged data are entered into the system, a "GIGO" situation may be created. This "input problem" is similar to the "output problem"—information overload. In order to design and develop more effective MISs, techniques should somehow be established to predict managerial information processing abilities and requirements, so that GIGO and information overload can be minimized, if not eliminated.

There is an increasing trend on the part of executives to interact with automated information storage and retrieval systems. In these "cybernated" systems, the manager and the information system are coupled together into a problem-solving network. Adaptability and flexibility in problem identification and definition, as well as access to both large amounts of data and computational power, are attributes of cybernated systems that enhance the utility of MIS console usage for managers. At present, it appears that the weak link in these cybernated systems is man—not the computer subsystem. In some instances, managers may feel threatened by these rigid, automated systems because of possible replacement or loss of status, and they may refuse to learn how to use them. They are also afraid of their "truncated, programmed, perspective."

Regarding manager-computer interface, the interactive relationship between the manager and the MIS is highly dependent on the nature of the equipment peripheral to the computer, the most popular and effective of which is the graphic display terminal. Managers seem to like this device because they find it easier to understand than other terminals. It can be used to facilitate the input-output styles not only of individual managers, but also of groups of managers. Although graphic terminals are a means of optimizing man-computer interaction, much work has also been done—and is continuing—in the utilization of more natural or conversational languages. Another critical consideration in the design of the MIS interface is "user reaction" and the process of making system attributes acceptable to users. Contributing to the spread of real-time MISs is improved computer technology, especially in computer-communications systems. The most salient advantage of real-time systems is their speed in processing information. Time-sharing terminals make it possible to have easy access to a central computer with its very short turn-around time. Thus, relatively efficient, noninterrupted, massed problem solving is possible. Yet some writers claim that the aura of scientific management that envelops the executive who has a computer terminal in his office may be somewhat illusory.

Lastly, regarding the future of manager-computer symbiosis, it seems that improved technology in communications, terminals, and switching systems will render impending information systems approximately parallel to the real information flow within the organization. That is, with the further development of these technical capabilities, organizations may be able to obtain parallel levels of information, allowing subordinates easy access to the same information that managers have. Unless time-sharing terminals are controlled or restricted, there is nothing to prevent the executive from being second-guessed by his underlings on nearly every decision. Also, according to some authors, what is required in terms of future research capability is a cost-effective means of studying user skills and individual differences in performance in man-computer communications and interacting computing. It may prove unnecessary to choose between man and computer; instead, man-computer systems may draw upon the unique capabilities of each—the human's talent for setting of goals, constructing hypotheses, and selecting criteria; the computer's ability rapidly to examine the alternatives.

Paradoxically, the impact of MIS on managerial performance and decision making has not been clearly established. In fact, the literature is full of contradictory data and ideas. Very little empirical research has been conducted and reported, and most of what appears contains unsubstantiated allegations, forecasts, or prognostications. Several authors claim that there are many perceived threats posed by MIS-initiated changes in the management environment. Others claim that there will be almost no impact at all on routine activities of management. In fact, though, present data are inadequate and cannot tell us what is actually the case. Further investigation is essential.

The literature is full of contradictory forecasts regarding the implications of MIS for the traditional functions of management. Ambiguity exists among the many allegations concerning the content and status of middle management's job. A few writers predict that MIS will have significant consequences for the job of management; others predict that the effects will not be significant at all, and that the MIS-produced "management revolution" will not occur. Which of these projections is correct? Again we lack sufficient data: further research is required.

Uncertainty also exists with respect to MDS and managerial decision making. Some individuals indicate that computerized systems will probably be programmed to mimic many of the complex decisions demanded of management. Other prognosticators assert that this will not be the case. Rather, they say, an irreducible number of irregular and critical decisions will still have to be made by the managers themselves. Once again, not enough empirical data exist to clarify this important problem area. Studies should be conducted that specifically address themselves to the consequences of MDSs for managerial decision making.

Is it in fact true that inadequate information systems "cannot be corrected by a computer"? It may be that attempting to automate information systems is the proper approach for solving communication problems of this kind. Much research needs to be done not only in this area, but also in the areas of natural language programming and conversational languages. More investigations should be performed, which attempt to identify what MIS attributes are acceptable to managers/users. Also, more work is required regarding the proper design of manager-computer systems, which attempt to optimize the idiosyncratic capabilities of each component.

If we are to enhance the aura of scientific management "which envelops the executive who has a computer terminal in his office," then we must energetically initiate research and development efforts to explore the exact empirical impact of MIS on managerial performance and decision making.

ORGANIZATIONAL STRUCTURE AND PROCESSES

For the most part MISs have been designed, developed, and implemented by firms with little understanding of the consequences for organizational structures and processes. It is not that effects are unanticipated or unexpected, for many writers recognize that the introduction of an MIS into an enterprise will generate substantial and sometimes radical changes within that organization. There is, however, hardly any agreement about what those effects will be. On the one hand, it is said that a trend toward more hourglass or pyramidal structures will develop; on the other hand, there is the expectation that organizational structures will be rearranged into shapes that are not as yet obvious.

The technological impact of MISs may necessitate the change of organizational structure in order to make explicit and to reinforce the relationship needed by the technology for maximal effectiveness. The new computerized procedures of information processing will be a salient factor in determining which new organizational forms are most appropriate and cost-effective. The MIS itself will become the heart of the organizational structure, the stabilizing force holding an enterprise together. Despite the many and varied opinions and predictions regarding the effects of MIS, there has been little objective and reliable data concerning its influence on organizational form. Instead of limited applications of MISs, more stress should be placed on redesigning entire organizational structures in order to match MISs that are being developed for use.

The greatest controversy surrounding MIS utilization concerns the tendency toward centralization. With the advent of MIS, the trend toward decentralization may be slowed, altered, or even reversed. MISs will also tend to reduce the number of levels within the organizational structure, as well as cause the regrouping of activities and the centralizing of control and authority. MISs may stimulate the recentralization of geographically dispersed decision centers, or recentralization of control over decision making.

An MIS may allow an increase in the range of tasks for which a particular subunit is responsible. Thus, the number of subunits comprising the organization can easily be reduced as each subunit's span of control increases. Obviously, the impact of MISs will not be identical in every organization. Many variables operate to accent, nullify, or even reverse the effects of MISs. Some evidence of recentralization has been cited in the literature. For the most part, however, such evidence is based on observations of organizational charts, job descriptions, computerized information systems, and employee interviews. Still, authoritarian or command structure may in fact shrink to a smaller number of levels. Consequently, many organizations may experience a reduction in the number of middle managers.

Yet still other studies give little support to the notion that greater centralization will occur in response to computer usage. Some authors have concluded, on the contrary, that a properly designed MIS is more conducive to organizational decentralization. They believe that the increasing utilization of MISs will neither seriously affect top management's control of operations, nor positively generate a trend to recentralize organizational structure. Computer technology may facilitate organizational decentralization and encourage a wider span of management. Additionally, the possibility exists that the impact of an MIS may be manipulated in order to reinforce or strengthen a firm's emphasis on decentralization. Top executives may be able to delegate even more decisions, because the system will provide them with a means to evaluate the performance of subordinates.

There are a number of situational factors that may in fact moderate or accentuate the interaction between computer technology and organizational structure. It is important to recognize the distinction between operations and control regarding the differential impact of an MIS on functional activities and the authority structure. That is, information-processing activities may be centralized without simultaneously altering the degree to which authority is either centralized or decentralized. With so many variables and factors confusing the issue, it is not surprising that considerable disagreement exists.

Some authors stress that an MIS is a system that affects only the control structure of an organization. Consequently, control must be considered in designing, implementing, and using information systems. A major advantage of an MIS is its ability to unify or integrate aspects of organizational operations into a unified control system. However, this function of MIS has not been appreciated and utilized nearly to the extent that it ought to be. As computerized information systems have been very important in providing top management with better control, the structural rules affecting manager's decision-making authority have loosened. However, according to some data, an MIS's capacity for better control results in tighter individual discipline at lower levels in the organization.

MISs are also likely to influence managerial style and motivation. In an organization where top management's control is being reinforced and centralization of structure is occurring, the motivation and performance of middle managers can suffer, especially if the shift in control toward the top is perceived as threatening the authority and accountability of these middle managers. There are other factors that may limit the impact of MISs on organizational control. Management problems are not merely more complex and difficult operational problems: operational activities can often be reported almost instantaneously by MIS, but higher level management problems tend to be less structured and programmable. A peculiar aspect of control that bears scrutiny is span of control. If an MIS causes decentralization, then span of control will probably decrease. This makes possible closer supervision and thus prevents mistakes and distortions in the transmission of information. It is possible, on the other hand, that an increase in the span of control will limit the need for middle managers.

An additional dimension of organizational structure that may be affected by an MIS has to do with delegation of authority. It appears that an MIS can make it possible for top-level executives to delegate authority to lower-level management without loss of control, because the MIS allows them to determine if the performance of subordinates deviates from acceptable standards. Often, an MIS is perceived as a key to power, an instrument that can be used by an executive to control the flow of critically important information. Control of the MIS is seen as vital in determining the distribution of power within the organization. It is likely that in the quick-responding, adaptive organization of the future, MISs will deemphasize the relationship between superior and subordinate, and emphasize the relationship between peers. These working partners will be organized around the need for pertinent information.

In addition to the general implications that MISs have for organizational behavior, the specific problems regarding organization of the computer systems department within the firm must also be considered. Such aspects as the internal structure of the department responsible for the computer system, the location of the MIS department within the organization, and the status of the system's management are all important facets of the organization's response to MIS usage. There is some indication that the efficiency of the MIS function may improve with the centralization of the information processing department.

While attempting to optimize an MIS's organizational effectiveness, top management should not overlook the problem of finding the best locus of control and responsibility for the MIS department. The consensus of opinion favors the establishment of an entirely independent information systems group. This unit should be directed by a specialist in computer and information systems, who reports directly to top management. Locating the information systems effort in an independent department is not without certain disadvantages, though, for while the staff of such a unit may have considerable expertise in computer and information technology, they may possess less than complete understanding of the needs and operations of the other departments comprising the organization.

At times, there is a strong tendency toward empire building on the part of MIS executives. As MIS applications expand throughout an organization, the functional responsibilities of other departments will be undercut and top management's authority truncated. However, although the MIS manager occupies a revered (yet ill-defined) position, he is still divorced from the primary center or organizational power. These MIS managers are isolated and insulated by their abilities and mystique. This walling-in inhibits communication, and, unlike the usurpation posture, may cause these managers to be ignored, by-passed, or allowed only trivial participation. The MIS manager is not the all-powerful information dictator. Yet the posture assumed by the MIS manager has important ramifications for the organization.

Organizational changes take place when MISs are introduced, implemented, and utilized within such a structure. Resistance to change is not a novel organizational problem. However, the introduction of MIS has added a new dimension to it. MIS-caused change creates conflict and stress, and in turn provokes resistance. In order to circumvent resistance, three techniques have been recommended: participation of those involved in the change; maintenance of open communications before, during, and after the change; and a combination form in which a committee oversees the change and utilizes both free communications and participation.

The introduction and utilization of MISs cause major lags in an organization's progress. This slowdown in growth is especially noticeable during the introduction or phasing-in stage of an MIS. Although the literature contains considerable information on the possible problems associated with MIS, few studies have been undertaken, or completed, concerning the actual results of such a change. In organizations where the MIS was installed to mimic simple tasks, the degree of change was practically nil. It appears, then, that organizational change may be directly related to the aims and means of the system.

Also of concern in evaluating the effects of MIS are the alterations projected and/or found in job content. One study establishes that the procedures were simplified when certain operations were consolidated by MIS. The literature implies that MIS will routinize jobs at the clerical level, enlarge them at the supervisory level, and do either at the managerial level. In addition to modifying task requirements, MIS will alter the skill levels needed to perform those requirements.

MIS will affect organizational jobs, related tasks, and required skills; it will affect, as well, the individual and his interpersonal relationships within the structure. Depersonalization may occur: a manager may perceive his role as an MIS-created niche reflecting only the requirements of the system—not the needs of the employee. With the introduction of an MIS, supervisors and older workers are likely to be especially hard hit by the projected and/or actual changes in their organizational environment. These individuals find it much more difficult to adapt to such changes than do younger employees.

Not all the authors reviewed here share this gloomy view. Some claim that the predicted displacement and domination of people by the computer has not occurred, and that MIS utilization does not necessarily lead to stress.

In short, the impact of MIS on the jobs, tasks, skills, and individuals of an organization has been prophesied, prognosticated, projected, and pondered, but few empirical studies have been undertaken to identify and describe the actual consequences of MIS use. Despite the abundance of information that has been generated, few conclusive statements can be made concerning the effects of installing and utilizing an MIS, because the salient components of MIS introduction and usage have not yet been clarified.

Some researchers have found that the installation of an MIS had a mixed impact on employment. Only a small percentage of the personnel were laid off as a direct result of the system: most were either transferred or left alone. Several authors single out clerical employees as that group most likely to feel the squeeze of MIS. It would seem that the traditional routines of clerical work are the most adaptable to MIS applications. However, other writers assert that there has been no significant reduction in the number of clerical employees on the economy level and few decreases within individual companies. MIS has actually slowed rather than reversed the rate of growth in clerical employment. Some data indicate that managerial manpower requirements will increase during transition to an MIS, but decrease as the system matures.

When an organization implements an MIS, a heretofore unknown set of interdepartmental interactions occurs. Two forms of organizational orientation have been attached to MIS utilization. One trend has been toward user-oriented systems. The technicians and programmers provide the basic facility, but they do not meddle in the interactions between the user and the facility. Users become extremely frustrated when they are bounced back and forth between programmers in their attempts to solve problems. Yet when the organization provides a liaison between the MIS and the user, satisfaction and confidence in the system increase.

If the organization assumes a technical orientation, whereby the user is given second priority behind the system and its mentors, another set of internal problems is created. Significant barriers to cooperative interaction arise. The user hopes to remain uninvolved with the MIS and thus effectively avoid being considered for the other system's "help." A solid barrier between management and MIS people exists because technicians speak a language management fails to understand—computer language. An implicit assumption of the literature is that the relationship of MIS specialist to line management should be organizationally defined.

It also appears that organizational communications are merging with computerized networks. This increased integration is probably due to demands for more timely information, more cost-effective data collection, and more technologically advanced systems for processing information. Computerized systems can change an organization's communication network, especially the development and dispersion of nonvertical information flow through the management structure. A newly designed and developed MIS may be incomplete as far as the real flow of information in the organization is concerned.

Another problem accompanying the implementation of MIS is the inversion of superior-subordinate relationships. It may be easier for a lower-level manager to program middle or top management if he has access to and control of an MIS terminal. Organizational entities such as chain-of-command, direct supervision, and mediated communication could easily be undermined by the utilization of an MIS, since face-to-face communication will likely decrease substantially and be replaced by direct interaction with a computerized information system.

Since upper management levels are usually remote from organizational resources, the greater the number of intermediate managers, the more probable the delays and distortions in the information flow. A computerized system can surmount these impediments by providing the technology to disseminate information more quickly and precisely through an organizational hierarchy. Such a system might even force on organizational members the use of a standardized language that would facilitate communications. Much of the information actually demanded by management concerns the organization's external environment. However, this is precisely the information not usually maintained within an MIS.

It seems that top-level managers find it very difficult to state clearly the precise characteristics of their informational demands, because of the global perspectives they possess of these external organizational environments. One of the primary advantages derived from utilizing an MIS is that computerized communication channels can be contoured to the actual flow of information within the organization. The proper, formal flow of information through a firm is the wherewithal of optimal decision making. Some of this problem-solving skill may be ascribed to the processes of selecting and filtering information, which is usually exercised prior to its inclusion in an MIS. This expeditious dissemination of information makes it possible to establish more uniform objectives throughout an organization.

An organization can be considered an information- and decision-processing framework, within which a manager serves as nodal information processor and decision maker. The flow of information through these individuals introduces intermittent time lags into the organizational network. The rate of information input and the time taken to make a decision usually specify the queuing effect ascribed to a single manager. A well-implemented MIS can (1) improve the effectiveness of this information processing and decision making by minimizing this queuing effect, and (2) surmount problems of information distortion attributed to typical interaction patterns between transmitters and receivers of information within organizations.

Another advantage of MIS is that organizational objectives can be explicitly stated and subjected to systematic analysis. This should improve the quality of organizational decision making.

However, not all events or outcomes attributed to MIS are completely profitable. It seems likely that the undisputed urge of subordinates to program managers to make decisions in a manner similar to that in which they are made by computers will intensify due to MIS utilization. In fact, top managers may not make decisions at all. Their discretionary powers may be truncated, usurped, and dictated by those who design, develop, and maintain the MIS.

Many authors claim that MIS centralizes the decision-making framework within the organization, and that the authority for making both structured and unstructured decisions will be allocated to nodal positions within the organization. Still other authors argue, on the contrary, that MIS will have a decentralizing effect on the decision-making structure. Just as easily as computerized systems can bring information to centrally located managers to improve their decision making, these systems can bring information to peripherally located managers to improve their decision making too. One consequence of this could be that peripheral personnel will have more discretionary responsibility, because they can now have access to the necessary information. In fact, though, neither trend has dominated the decision-making environment. Computerized information systems will probably increase the importance of group decision making and the tendency toward greater risk taking. It remains to be seen, however, whether or not the speed and precision of the information provided by MISs, together with this shift toward more riskiness, will produce better decisions.

The total organization is considered a complete communication system whose information flows are funneled through nodal decision makers in order to improve their performance. Often, communication networks are completely reconfigured by integrated MISs to facilitate the flow of information. It would be wise to plan an integrated system not only to combine the numerous decision nodes in an information network, but also to include the information requirements of different organizational levels. Still, several authors are very skeptical regarding the successful development and implementation of integrated MISs. The incompatibility of many of the components contributes to the difficulty of establishing integrated systems.

In light of the enormous expense of computerized systems, it is astonishing how skimpy the research is concerning MIS design. It seems that no methodical or universal theory exists that is adequate for the proper planning of MISs. However, some specific standards have been established, which should form the basis of MIS design. It would be a gross error to plan an MIS without complete concern for the human factor. After all is said and done, this is the dimension that ultimately determines whether or not an MIS will be successful. A number of personnel, each of whom possesses a specific expertise, must be involved in the design and development of MISs because of the complexity, differentiation, and federation of many information systems required in an integrated system.

It seems improbable that an effective MIS could be created by following the flow of a firm's existing information network. Theoretically, it is much better to plan an MIS apart from the firm's existing system. In order to design an effective MIS, it is necessary to specify in advance crucial decision nodes in the network, so that information can be channeled to reach the proper people for discretionary purposes. In addition, an MIS should be designed to yield not

Baker, J. D. Quantitative modelling of human performance in information systems. Ergonomics, 1970, 13, 645-664.

Balk, W. L. The human dilemmas of MIS. Journal of Systems Management, 1971, 22(8), 35-38.

Baran, P. Communications, computers and people (P-3235). Santa Monica, Calif.: The Rand Corporation, November 1965.

Barnett, J. H. Non-computer executives and the computer. Journal of Systems Management, 1969, 20(12), 14-22.

Bassett, G. A. EDP personnel systems: Do's, don'ts, and how-to's. Personnel, 1971, 48(4), 19-27.

Baum, B., & Burack, E. Information technology, manpower development and organizational performance. Academy of Management Journal, 1969, 12(3), 279-291.

Becker, R. T. Training to use the computer as an executive tool. Personnel, 1970, 47(6), 36-41.

Becker, S. W., & Baloff, N. Organization structure and complex problem solving. Administrative Science Quarterly, 1969, 14(2), 260-271.

Beckett, J. A. Management, motivation, and management information systems. Advanced Management Journal, 1965, 30(1), 66-73.

Beged-Dov, A. G. An overview of management science and information systems. Management Science, 1967, 13(12), B817-B831.

Benne, K. D., & Birnbaum, M. Principles of changing. In W. G. Bennis, K. D. Benne, & R. Chin (Eds.), The planning of change. New York: Holt, Rinehart and Winston, 1969.

Bennis, W. G. New patterns of leadership for tomorrow's organizations. Technology Review, April 1968.

Berkowitz, N., & Munro, R., Jr. Automatic data processing and management. Belmont, Calif.: Dickenson, 1969.

Berkwitt, G. Middle managers vs. the computer. Dun's Review, 1966, 88(5), 40-42; 107-110.

Berkwitt, G. J. The new executive elite. Dun's Review, 1971, 98(1), 25-27.

Bieneman, J. N. Bridging the gap between data processing and operating departments: A fresh approach. Management Advisor, 1972, 9(5), 17-20.

Birks, E. G. The computer in a management information system. In W. C. House (Ed.), The impact of information technology on management operations. New York: Auerbach, 1971.

Blose, W. F., & Goetze, E. E. On-line processing—How will it affect your organizational structure? In W. C. House (Ed.), The impact of information technology on management operation. New York: Auerbach, 1971.

Boettinger, H. M. The impact of technology. In P. F. Drucker (Ed.), Preparing tomorrow's business leaders today. Englewood Cliffs, N.J.: Prentice-Hall, 1969.

Boulden, J. B., & Buffa, E. S. Corporate models: On-line, real-time systems. Harvard Business Review, 1970, 48(4), 65-83.

Brabb, G. J., & Hutchins, E. B. Electronic computers and management organization. California Management Review, 1963, 6(1), 33-42.

Brady, R. H. Computers in top-level decision making. Harvard Business Review, 1967, 45(4), 67-76.

Bright, J. R. Opportunity and threat in technological change. Harvard Business Review, 1963, 41(6), 76-86.

Brill, A. E. The alienation of the system analyst. Journal of Systems Management, 1974, 25(1), 26-29.

Burck, G. The age of the computer: Management will never be the same. Management Review, 1964, 53(9), 16-20. (a)

Burck, G. The boundless age of the computer. Fortune, March 1964, 101-110. (b)

Burdeau, H. B. Environmental approach to MIS. Journal of Systems Management, 1974, 25(4), 11-13.

Burlingame, J. F. Information technology and decentralization. Harvard Business Review, 1961, 39(6), 121-126.

Carlson, J. G. H., & Gilman, R. Less data—more information. Paper presented at the meeting of the Western Division of the Academy of Management, San Francisco, April 1974.

Carroll, D. C. Man-machine cooperation on planning and control problems. Industrial Management Review, 1966, 8(1), 45-54.

Carroll, D. C. Implications of on-line, real-time systems for managerial decision-making. In C. A. Myers (Ed.), The impact of computers on management. Cambridge, Mass.: M.I.T. Press, 1967.

Cattaneo, E. R. Executives dissatisfied with EDP activities. Computer Digest, 1971, 6(12), 1.

Churchill, N. C., Kempster, J. H., & Uretsky, M. Computer-based information systems for management: A survey. New York: National Association of Accountants, 1969.

Clayton, E. R. Management information systems—corporate life. Advanced Management Journal, 1973, 38(1), 54-59.

Coiner, L. M. EDPerspective. Administrative Management, 1973, 34(4), 14.

Coleman, R. J., & Riley, M. J. The organizational impact of MIS. Journal of Systems Management, 1972, 23(3), 13-19.

Computers and middle management. Administrative Management, 1966, 27(6), 19.

Conomikes, G. Computers are creating personnel problems. Personnel Journal, 1967, 46, 52-53.

Cooper, R., & Foster, M. Sociotechnical systems. American Psychologist, 1971, 26(5), 467-474.

Crowley, W. J. Can we integrate systems without integrating management? Journal of Data Processing, August 1966.

Cyert, R. M., Simon, H. A., & Trow, D. B. Observation of a business decision. Journal of Business, 1956, 24(4), 237-248.

Dale, E. The decision-making process in the commercial use of high-speed computers. Ithaca, N.Y.: Graduate School of Business and Public Administration, Cornell University, 1964.

Daniel, D. R. Management information crisis. Harvard Business Review, 1961, 39(5), 111-121.

Daniel, D. R. Reorganizing for results. Harvard Business Review, 1966, 44(6), 96-104.

Dean, N. J. The computer comes of age. Harvard Business Review, 1968, 46(1), 83-91.

Dearden, J. Can management information be automated? Harvard Business Review, 1964, 42(2), 128-135.

Dearden, J. How to organize information systems. Harvard Business Review, 1965, 43(2), 65-73.

Dearden, J. Myth of real-time management information. Harvard Business Review, 1966, 44(3), 123-132.

Dearden, J. Computers: No impact on divisional control. Harvard Business Review, 1967, 45(1), 99-104.

Dearden, J. MIS is a mirage. Harvard Business Review, 1972, 50(1), 90-99.

Delehanty, G. E. Office automation and the occupation structure. Industrial Management Review, 1966, 7(2), 99-108.

Dickson, G. W. Management information—decision systems. Business Horizons, 1968, 11(6), 17-26.

Diebold, J. What's ahead in information technology. Management Review, 1965, 54(10), 52-56.

Diebold, J. Bad decisions on computer use. Harvard Business Review, 1969, 47(1), 13-16; 27-28; 176. (a)

Diebold, J. The information revolution. In P. F. Drucker (Ed.), Preparing tomorrow's business leaders today. Englewood Cliffs, N.J.: Prentice-Hall, 1969. (b)

Dobelis, M. C. The three-day week—offshoot of an EDP operation. Personnel, 1972, 49(1), 24-33.

Dock, V. T.; Luchsinger, V. P.; & Cornette, W. R. (Eds.). MIS: A managerial perspective. Chicago: Science Research Associates, 1977.

Dreyfus, H. Alchemy and artificial intelligence. (Technical Memorandum). Santa Monica, Calif.: The Rand Corporation, 1965.

Driver, M. J., & Streufert, S. Integrative complexity: An approach to individuals and groups as information-processing systems. Administrative Science Quarterly, 1969, 14(2), 272-285.

Drucker, P. F. The practice of management. New York: Harper and Row, 1954.

Drucker, P. F. Managing the educated. In D. H. Fenn (Ed.), Management's mission in a new society. New York: McGraw-Hill, 1956.

Drucker, P. F. What computers will be telling you. Management Review, 1966, 55(10), 30-33.

Drucker, P. F. The manager and the moron. Management Review, 1967, 56(7), 20-26.

Edwards, W., & Slovic, P. Seeking information to reduce the risk of decisions. American Journal of Psychology, 1965, 78, 188-197.

Eilon, S. Some notes on information processing. The Journal of Management Studies, 1968, 5(2), 139-153.

Eilon, S. What is a decision? Management Science, 1969, 16(4), B172-B189.

Ein-Dor, P. Parallel strategy for MIS. Journal of Systems Management, 1975, 26(3), 30-35.

Elliott, C. What managers can do to break the EDP barrier. Administrative Management, 1974, 35(1), 50.

Elliott, J. D. EDP—its impact on jobs, procedures and people. The Journal of Industrial Engineering, 1958, 9(5), 407-410.

Emery, J. C. The impact of information technology on organizations. In W. C. House (Ed.), The impact of information technology on management operation. New York: Auerbach, 1971.

Ensign, R. B. Measuring the flow of management information. The Journal of Systems Management, 1974, 25(2), 40-43.

Ernst, M. L. Computers, business and society. Management Review, 1970, 59(11), 4-12.

Evans, M. K., & Hague, L. R. Master plan for information systems. Harvard Business Review, 1962, 40(1), 92-103.

Fayol, H. [General and industrial management.] (J. A. Conbrough, trans.). Geneva: International Management Institute, 1929. (Originally published, 1922.)

Field, G. A. Behavioral aspects of the computer. MSU Business Topics, 1970, 18(3), 27-33.

Finn, K. R., & Miller, H. B. Is your MIS fit for human consumption? Industrial Engineering, 1971, 3(11), 18-20.

Fiock, L. R. Seven deadly dangers in EDP. Harvard Business Review, 1962, 40(2), 88-96.

Fisch, G. G. Stretching the span of management. Harvard Business Review, 1963, 41(4), 74-85.

Fredericks, W. A. A manager's perspective of management information systems. MSU Business Topics, 1971, 19(1), 7-12.

Fried, L. S., & Peterson, C. R. Information seeking: Optional versus fixed stopping. Journal of Experimental Psychology, 1969, 80(3), 525-529.

Gallagher, C. A. Perceptions of the value of a management information system. Academy of Management Journal, 1974, 17(1), 46-55.

Garrity, J. T. Top management and computer profits. Harvard Business Review, 1963, 41(4), 6-8; 10; 12; 172; 174.

Gerrity, T. P. Design of man-machine decision systems. Sloan Management Review, 1971, 12(2), 59-75.

Gibson, C. F., & Nolan, R. L. Managing the four stages of EDP growth. Harvard Business Review, 1974, 52(1), 76-88.

Gilman, G. The computer revisited. Business Horizons, 1966, 9(4), 77-89.

Goldston, E. The limits of technology. In D. W. Ewing (Ed.), Technological change and management. Cambridge, Mass.: Harvard University Press, 1970.

Greenless, M. Time-sharing computers in business. In W. C. House, The impact of information technology on management operation. New York: Auerbach, 1971.

Greenbaum, H. H. The audit of organizational communication. Academy of Management Journal, 1974, 17(4), 739-754.

Greenwood, W. T. Decision theory and information systems. Chicago: South-Western, 1969.

Greenwood, W. T. Future management theory: A "comparative" evolution to a general theory. Academy of Management Journal, 1974, 17(3), 503-513.

Greiner, L. E., Leitch, D. P., & Barnes, L. B. Putting judgment back into decisions. Harvard Business Review, 1970, 48(2), 59-67.

Haberstroh, C. J. The impact of electronic data processing on administrative organizations. National Tax Journal, 1961, 14, 258-270.

Hanold, T. A president's view of MIS. Datamation, November 1968, pp. 59-62.

Head, R. V. Management information systems: A critical appraisal. Datamation, May 1967, pp. 22-27.

Hershman, A. A mess in MIS? Dun's Review, 1968, 91(1), 26-27; 85-87.

Hill, L. S. Communications, semantics, and information systems. The Journal of Industrial Engineering, 1965, 16(2), 131-135.

Hill, W. A. The impact of EDP systems on office employees: Some empirical conclusions. Academy of Management Journal, 1966, 9(3), 9-19.

Hirsch, R. E. The value of information. The Journal of Accountancy, June 1968, 41-45.

Hofer, C. W. Emerging EDP pattern. Harvard Business Review, 1970, 48(2), 16-31; 169-171.

Holland, W. E., Kretlow, W. J., & Ligon, J. C. Sociotechnical aspects of MIS. Journal of Systems Management, 1974, 25(2), 14-16.

Holmes, R. W. 12 areas to investigate for better MIS. Financial Executive, 1970, 38(7), 24-31.

Hoos, I. R. When the computer takes over the office. Harvard Business Review, 1960, 38(4), 102-112.

Hoos, I. R. Information systems and public planning. Management Science, 1971, 17(10), B658-B671.

Horton, F. W., Jr. The evolution of MIS in government. Journal of Systems Management, 1974, 25(3), 14-20.

How the computer is changing management organization. Business Management, 1967, 32(4), 26-30.

Ignizio, J. P., & Shannon, R. E. Organization structures in the 1980's. Industrial Engineering, 1971, 3(9), 46-50.

Jackson, R. S. Computers and middle management. Journal of Systems Management, 1970, 21(4), 22-24.

Jasinski, F. J. Adapting organization to new technology. Harvard Business Review, 1959, 37(1), 79-86.

Jayant, P. EDP is dead; long live EDP. Journal of Systems Management, 1974, 25(11), 18-23.

Johnson, R. L., & Derman, I. H. How intelligent is your "MIS"? Business Horizons, 1970, 13(1), 55-62.

Johnson, R. A., Fremont, E. K., & Rosenzweig, J. The theory and management of systems. New York: McGraw-Hill, 1963.

Jones, C. H. At last: Real computer power for decision makers. Harvard Business Review, 1970, 48(5), 75-89.

Jordan, N. Motivational problems in human-computer operations. Human Factors, 1962, 4(3), 171-175.

Joseph, E. C. The coming age of management information systems. In W. C. House (Ed.), The impact of information technology on management operation. New York: Auerbach, 1971.

Kadin, M. B., & Green, R. Computerization in the medium-sized CPA firm. The Journal of Accountancy, 1971, 74(2), 44-49.

Kanter, J. Management-oriented management information systems. Englewood Cliffs, N.J.: Prentice-Hall, 1972.

Karp, W. Management's future role: Picking up where the computer leaves off. Management Review, 1971, 60(3), 14-17.

Kaufman, H. G. Job design and adjustment to computer automation. Journal of Industrial Psychology, 1965, 3(3), 61-67.

Keegan, W. J. Multinational scanning: A study of the information sources utilized by headquarters executives in multinational companies. Administrative Science Quarterly, 1974, 19(3), 411-421.

Kegerreis, R. J. Marketing management and the computer: An overview of conflict and contrast. Journal of Marketing, 1971, 35, 3-12.

Keller, A. F. EDP—Power in search of management. Business Automation, 1966, 13(6), 48-52.

Kennevan, W. J. MIS universe. Data Management, 1970, 8(9), 62-64.

Klahr, D., & Leavitt, H. J. Tasks, organization structures, and computer programs. In C. A. Myers (Ed.), The impact of computers on management. Cambridge, Mass.: M.I.T. Press, 1967.

Kleinschrod, W. A. Computers and middle management: Where are we now? Administrative Management, 1969, 30(5), 20-23.

Koontz, H. Top management takes a second look at electronic data processing. Business Horizons, 1959, 2(1), 74-84.

Krauss, L. I. Computer-based management information systems. New York: American Management Association, 1970.

Kraut, A. I. How EDP is affecting workers and organizations. Personnel, 1962, 39(4), 38-50.

Kunreuther, H. Extensions of Bowan's theory on managerial decision-making. Management Science, 1969, 15(8), B415-B439.

Kurz, R. C. Long live the data administrator. Datamation, March 1973, 72-74.

Kushner, A. People and computers. Personnel, 1963, 40(1), 27-34.

Lanzetta, J. T., & Kanareff, V. T. Information cost, amount of payoff, and level of aspiration as determinants of information seeking in decision making. Behavioral Science, 1962, 7(2), 459-473.

Leavitt, H. J., & Whisler, T. L. Management in the 1980's. Harvard Business Review, 1958, 36(6), 41-48.

Lee, H. C. On information technology and organization structure. Academy of Management Journal, 1964, 7(3), 204-210.

Lee, H. C. Do workers really want flexibility on the job? Personnel, 1965, 42(2), 74-77.

Lee, H. C. The organizational impact of computers. Management Services, 1967, 4(3), 39-43.

Lipstreu, O. Organizational implications of automation. Academy of Management Journal, 1960, 3(2), 119-124.

Lucas, H. C. Computer based information systems in organizations. Chicago: Science Research Associates, Inc., 1973.

McDonough, A. M. Information economics and management systems. New York: McGraw-Hill, 1963.

McDonough, A. M. Keys to a management information system in your company. In The third generation computer. New York: American Management Association, 1966.

McFarland, R. L. Electronic power grab. In P. Schoderbek (Ed.), Management Systems (2nd ed.). New York: John Wiley & Sons, 1971.

McGregor, D. M. The human side of enterprise. In E. A. Fleishman & A. R. Bass (Eds.), Studies in Personnel Psychology. Homewood, Ill.: Dorsey Press, 1974.

Mahoney, T. A., Jerdee, T. H., & Carroll, S. J. The job(s) of management. Industrial Relations, 1965, 4(2), 97-110.

Malcolm, D. G., & Rowe, A. J. An approach to computer-based management control systems. California Management Review, 1961, 3(3), 4-15.

Mann, F. C., & Williams, L. K. Observations on the dynamics of a change to electronic data-processing equipment. Administrative Science Quarterly, 1960, 5(1), 217-256.

Marquis, D. G. Individual responsibility and group decisions involving risk. Industrial Management Review, 1962, 3, 8-23.

Martin, E. W. Electronic data processing. Homewood, Ill.: Richard D. Irwin, 1965.

Mayer, S. J. EDP personnel systems: What areas are being automated? Personnel, 1971, 48(4), 29-36.

Mayer, S. R. Trends in human factors research for military information systems. Human Factors, 1970, 12(2), 177-186.

Megginson, L. C. Automation: Our greatest asset—our greatest problem. Academy of Management Journal, 1963, 6(3), 232-244.

Melitz, P. W. Impact of electronic data processing on managers. Advanced Management, 1961, 26(1), 4-6.

Melly, F. J. Report on the computer backlash. Advanced Manage-Journal, 1974, 49(4), 10-14.

Meyer, M. W. Automation and bureaucratic structure. American Journal of Sociology, 1968, 74(3), 256-264.

Miller, G. A. The magical number seven, plus or minus two: Some limits on our capacity for processing information. The Psychological Review, 1956, 63(2), 81-97.

Miller, G. A. Computer, communication, and cognition. The Advancement of Science, 1965, 21(93), 417-430.

Miller, I. M. Computer graphics for decision making. Harvard Business Review, 1969, 47(6), 121-132.

Miner, J. B. Management theory. New York: Macmillan, 1971.

Mitroff, I. I. Personal communication, March 7, 1975.

Moan, F. E. Does management practice lag behind theory in the computer environment? Academy of Management Journal, 1973, 16(1), 7-23.

Moravec, A. F. Basic concepts for planning advanced electronic data processing systems. Management Services, 1965, 2(3), 52-60.

Morton, M. S., & McCosh, A. M. Terminal costing for better decisions. Harvard Business Review, 1968, 46(3), 147-156.

Morton, M. S. S. Management decision systems. Boston, Mass.: Harvard University, Graduate School of Business Administration, Division of Research, 1971.

Mulder, M. Communication structure, decision structure and group performance. Sociometry, 1960, 23(1), 1-14.

Mumford, E., & Ward, T. Computer technologists—dilemmas of a new role. Journal of Management Studies, 1966, 3(3), 244-255.

Murdick, R. G., & Ross, J. E. Future management information systems—part II. Journal of Systems Management, 1972, 23(5), 32-35.

National Bureau of Standards (NBS). Training for automation and information processing in the federal service. Washington, D.C.: U.S. National Bureau of Standards, 1966.

Neel, C. W. Counter conduct in mechanical systems. Journal of Systems Management, 1971, 22(12), 35-38.

Neuschel, R. F. Management by systems. New York: McGraw-Hill, 1960.

A new look in management reporting. EDP Analyzer, 1965, 3(6), 1-15.

Nicholoson, S. The bright young men of information. Dun's Review and Modern Industry, 1963, 82(Pt. 2), 96-146.

Nickerson, R. S., Elkind, J. I., & Carbonell, J. R. Human factors and the design of time sharing computer systems. Human Factors, 1968, 10(2), 127-134.

Northrup, G. M. Digital communications and EDP for an advanced tactical air control systems: A preliminary study. (RM-4431-PR). Santa Monica, Calif.: The Rand Corporation, January 1965.

O'Brien, J. A. How computers have changed the organizational structure. Banking, 1968, 61(1), 43-45.

Osmond, C. N. Corporate planning: Its impact on management. Long Range Planning, 1971, 3(3), 34-40.

Orlicky, J. The successful computer system. New York: McGraw-Hill, 1969.

An overview of the information processing and computer community. Journal of Data Management, 1969, 7(6), 20-38.

Parsons, R. B. The impact of the computer on management principles. Advanced Management Journal, 1968, 33(10), 51-53.

Pattillo, J. W. A study in instant information. Management Accounting, 1969, 50(9), 17-20.

Peace, D. M. S., & Easterby, R. S. The evaluation of user interaction with computer-based management information systems. Human Factors, 1973, 15(2), 163-177.

People and machines: The delicate balance. Personnel Journal, 1974, 53(5), 374-375.

Petroff, J. N. Why are DP managers so unpopular? Datamation, February 1973, 77-79.

Pettigrew, A. Inter-group conflict and role strain. Journal of Management Studies, 1968, 5(2), 205-218.

Poindexter, J. The information specialist: From data to dollars. Dun's Review, 1969, 93(6), 34-37.

Porter, L. W., & Ghiselli, E. E. The self perceptions of top and middle management personnel. Personnel Psychology, 1957, 10(4), 397-406.

Porter, W. T., Jr., & Mulvihill, D. E. Organization for effective information flow. Management Services, 1965, 2(6), 13-20.

Powers, R. F., & Dickson, G. S. MISProject management: Myths, opinions, and reality. California Management Review, 1973, 15(3), 147-156.

Pryor, L. Time sharing at this point in time. Journal of Data Management, 1969, 7(5), 30-32.

Rader, L. T. Will management be automated by 1975? Management Science, 1968, 14(7), A720-A727.

Radford, K. J. Information systems in management. Reston, Va.: Reston, 1973.

Ransdell, W. K. Managing the people who manage the computer. Journal of Systems Management, 1975, 26(9), 18-21.

Rapoport, A. Sequential decision-making in a computer-controlled task. Journal of Mathematical Psychology, 1964, 1, 351-374.

Reif, W. E. Computer technology and management organization. Iowa City: University of Iowa Press, 1968.

Reynolds, W. H. The executive synecdoche. MSU Business Topics, 1969, 17(4), 21-29.

Rogers, E. M., & Shoemaker, F. F. Communication of innovations. New York: The Free Press, 1971.

Ross, J. E. Management information. Englewood Cliffs, N.J.: Prentice-Hall, 1970.

Rowe, A. J. Management by computer . . . how and when? Aerospace Management, 1961, 4(10), 66-72.

Rowe, A. J. Management decision making and the computer. Management International, 1962, (2), 9-22.

Sackman, H. Experimental analysis of man-computer problem-solving. Human Factors, 1970, 12(2), 187-201.

Sage, D. M. Information systems: A brief look into history. Datamation, November 1968, 63-69.

Sanders, D. H. Personnel management approaches of small firms to the change to EDP. Advanced Management Journal, 1966, 31(10), 56-61.

Sanders, D. H. Computers, organization, and managers: Some questions and speculations. Advanced Management Journal, 1969, 34(7), 72-77.

Schewe, C. D. The forgotten man. Journal of Systems Management, 1973, 24(1), 30-33.

Schoderbek, P. P. Management systems (2nd ed.). New York: John Wiley & Sons, 1971.

Schoderbek, P. P., & Babcock, J. D. The proper placement of computers and management involvement in EDP. In P. Schoderbek (Ed.), Management Systems (2nd ed.). New York: John Wiley & Sons, 1971.

Schoderbek, P. P., & Schoderbek, S. E. Integrated information systems—shadow or substance? Management Advisor, 1971, 8(6), 27-32.

Schroder, H., Driver, M., & Streufert, S. Human information processing. New York: Holt, Rinehart and Winston, 1967.

Schwitter, J. P. Computer effects upon managerial jobs. Academy of Management Journal, 1965, 8(3), 233-236.

Seese, D. A. Initiating a total information system. Journal of Systems Management, 1970, 21(4), 33-38.

Shaul, D. R. What's really ahead for middle management. Personnel, 1964, 41(6), 8-16.

Shaw, M. E. Some effects of problem complexity upon problem solution efficiency in different communication nets. Journal of Experimental Psychology, 1954, 48, 211-217. (a)

Shaw, M. E. Some effects of unequal distribution of information upon group performance in various communication nets. Journal of Abnormal and Social Psychology, 1954, 49, 547-553. (b)

Shaw, M. E. Group dynamics: The psychology of small group behavior. New York: McGraw-Hill, 1971.

Shott, G. L., Albright, L. E., & Glennon, J. R. Predicting turnover in an automated office situation. Personnel Psychology, 1963, 16, 213-219.

Simon, H. A. Centralization and decentralization in organizing the controllers' department. Carnegie Institute of Technology, Graduate School of Industrial Administration, 1954.

Simon, H. A. The corporation: Will it be managed by machines? In M. Anshen & G. L. Bach (Eds.), Management and corporations 1985. New York: McGraw-Hill, 1960. (a)

Simon, H. A. Management by machine. Management Review, 1960, 44(11), 12-19; 68-80. (b)

Simon, H. A. The new science of management decision. New York: Harper & Row, 1960. (c)

Simon, H. A. Will the corporation be managed by machines? In H. A. Simon, The shape of automation for men and management. New York: Harper & Row, 1965.

Simon, H. A. Reflections on time sharing from a user's point of view. Computer Science Research Review, Carnegie Institute of Technology, 1966, 43-51.

Simon, H. A. Information can be managed. Think, 1967, 33(3), 9-12.

Slater, R. E. Sixty-second man in a pico-second world. Management Thinking, July 1967, pp. 28-32.

Slovic, P. From Shakespeare to Simon: Speculations—and some evidence—about man's ability to process information. ORI Research Monograph, 1972, 12(2).

Slovic, P., Fleissner, D., & Bauman, W. S. Analyzing the use of information in investment decision making: A methodological proposal. The Journal of Business of the University of Chicago, 1972, 45(2), 283-301.

Sprague, R. H., Jr., & Watson, H. J. MIS concepts: Part 1. Journal of Systems Management, 1975, 26(1), 34-37. (a)

Sprague, R. H., Jr., & Watson, H. J. MIS concepts: Part II. Journal of Systems Management, 1975, 26(2), 35-40. (b)

Stern, H. Management information system—what it is and why. Management Science, 1970, 17(2), B119-B123.

Stern, H. Human relations and information systems. The Bulletin, 1971, 1(2), 39-43.

Stern, H. Information systems in management science. Interfaces, 1972, 3(1), 18-20. (a)

Stern, H. Is information systems talking to itself? Interfaces, 1972, 2(4), 54-57. (b)

Stewart, R. How computers affect management. Cambridge, Mass.: M.I.T. Press, 1971.

Stewart, T. R., West, R. E., Hammond, K. R., & Kreith, F. Improving human judgement in technology assessment. Journal of the International Society for Technology Assessment, 1975, 1(2).

Stieber, J. Automation and the white-collar worker. Personnel, 1957, 34(6), 8-17.

Swart, J. C., & Baldwin, R. A. EDP effects on clerical workers. Academy of Management Journal, 1971, 14(4), 497-512.

Taylor, J. W., & Dean, N. J. Managing to manage the computer. Harvard Business Review, 1966, 44(6), 78-110.

Taylor, R. N. Age and experience as determinants of managerial information processing and decision making performance. Academy of Management Journal, 1975, 18(1), 74-81.

Tetz, F. F. Evaluating computer-based human resource information systems: Cost vs. benefits. Personnel Journal, 1973, 52, 451-455.

Thompson, V. A. Hierarchy, specialization, and organizational conflict. Administrative Science Quarterly, 1961, 5, 485-521.

Thurston, P. H. Who should control information systems? Harvard Business Review, 1962, 40(1), 135-139.

Uris, A. Middle management and technological change. Management Review, 1963, 52(10), 55-58. (a)

Uris, A. What's ahead for middle management? Chemical Engineering, August 19, 1963, pp. 176-180. (b)

Vandell, R. F. Management evolution in the quantitative world. Harvard Business Review, 1970, 48(1), 83-92.

Vaughan, V. A. Plan for project success. Journal of Systems Management, 1974, 25(12), 12-15.

Vazsonyi, A. The use of mathematics in production and inventory control. Management Science, 1954, 1(1), 7-15.

Vazsonyi, A. Semantic pollution in information systems. Interfaces, 1973, 3(4), 43-46. (a)

Vazsonyi, A. Why should the management scientist grapple with information systems. Interfaces, 1973, 3(2), 1-18. (b)

Vazsonyi, A. Pragmatics: Rational approach to irrationality. Interfaces, 1974, 4(3), 40-45.

Vergin, R. C. Computer induced organization changes. MSU Business Topics, 1967, 15(2), 61-68.

Vergin, R. C., & Grimes, A. J. Management myths and EDP. California Management Review, 1964, 7(1), 59-70.

Walker, C. R. Basic human problems in mass-production technologies: Pacing, pressure, and repetitiveness. In C. R. Walker (Ed.), Technology, industry and man. New York: McGraw-Hill, 1968.

Wallach, M. A., & Kogan, N. The roles of information, discussion, and consensus in group risk taking. Journal of Experimental Social Psychology, 1965, 1, 1-19.

Wallach, M. A., Kogan, N., & Bem, D. J. Group influence on individual risk taking. Journal of Abnormal and Social Psychology, 1962, 65(2), 75-86.

Weber, C. E. Change in managerial manpower with mechanization of data-processing. The Journal of Business, 1959, 32, 151-163.

West, G. M. MIS in small companies. Journal of Systems Management, 1975, 26(4), 10-13.

Whisler, T. L. Measuring centralization of control in business organizations. In W. W. Cooper, H. J. Leavitt, & M. S. Shelly II (Eds.), New perspectives in organization research. New York: John Wiley & Sons, 1964.

Whisler, T. L. The manager and the computer. The Journal of Accountancy, 1965, 122, 27-32.

Whisler, T. L. Impact of information technology on organizational control. In C. A. Myers (Ed.), The impact of computers on management. Cambridge, Mass.: M.I.T. Press, 1967.

Whisler, T. L. The impact of computers on organizations. New York: Praeger, 1970. (a)

Whisler, T. L. Information technology and organizational change. Belmont, Calif.: Wadsworth, 1970. (b)

Whisler, T. L., & Shultz, G. P. Information technology and management organization. In G. P. Shultz & T. L. Whisler (Eds.), Management organization and the computer. Glencoe, Ill.: The Free Press of Glencoe, 1960.

Whisler, T. L., & Shultz, G. P. Automation and the management process. The Annals of the American Academy of Political and Social Science, 1962, 340, 81-89.

Wilkinson, J. W. Guidelines for designing systems. Journal of Systems Management, 1974, 25(12), 36-40.

Williams, L. K. The human side of a systems change. In P. Schoderbek (Ed.), Management Systems (2nd ed.). New York: John Wiley & Sons, 1971.

Williams, L. K., & Williams, C. B. The impact of numerically controlled equipment on factory organization. California Management Review, 1964, 7(2), 25-34.

Wynne, B. E., & Dickson, G. W. Experienced managers' performance in experimental man-machine decision system simulation. Academy of Management Journal, 1975, 18(1), 25-40.

Yaffa, E., & Hines, P. Who should control the computer. Management Review, 1969, 58(3), 2-11.

Yntema, D. B., & Torgerson, W. S. Man-computer cooperation in decisions requiring common sense. IRE Transactions on Human Factors in Electronics, 1961, HFE-2(1), 20-26.

Zald, M. N. Decentralization—myth vs. reality. Personnel, 1964, 41(4), 19-26.

Zani, W. M. Blueprint for MIS. Harvard Business Review, 1970, 48(6), 95-100.

Zannetos, Z. S. On the theory of divisional structures: Some aspects of centralization and decentralization of control and decision making. Management Science, 1965, 12(4), B49-B67.

Ziller, R. C. Four techniques of group decision making under uncertainty. Journal of Applied Psychology, 1957, 41, 384-388.

INDEX

ABOUT THE AUTHORS

PAT-ANTHONY FEDERICO is a research psychologist at the Navy Personnel Research and Development Center, San Diego, California. He received his Ph.D. in general experimental psychology from Tulane University in 1969, and has research interests in several aspects of human information processing and sociotechnical systems, including the implications of computer-managed informational and instructional systems. He has contributed articles to various journals, such as the Journal of Experimental Psychology, Personnel Psychology, Journal of Social Psychology, Journal of General Psychology, and Psychological Reports.

KIM E. BRUN is a graduate student at San Diego State University in business administration, and a research analyst for the San Diego State Foundation. He is concerned with the practice of management and how this is affected by information technology.

DOUGLAS B. McCALLA has just completed a graduate program in organizational and industrial psychology at San Diego State University. He is interested in the organizational implications of computerized information systems. He was also a research analyst for the San Diego State University Foundation.